LIVING LITURGY™

for Extraordinary Ministers of Holy Communion

Year C • 2025

George J. Doyle
Katharine E. Harmon
Jessica Mannen Kimmet
Barbara E. Reid, OP
Matthew Sherman
Michele Dachtler Warner

LITURGICAL PRESS
Collegeville, Minnesota

litpress.org

Cover design by Monica Bokinskie. Art by Ruberval Monteiro da Silva, OSB.

Closing prayer by John T. Kyler.

ISSN 1933-3129

ISBN 979-8-4008-0056-6

Presented to

____

in grateful appreciation
for ministering as an
Extraordinary Minister
of
Holy Communion

____

____

(date)

USING THIS RESOURCE

Extraordinary typically refers to outstanding or exceptional. But extraordinary ministers of Holy Communion are "extra"ordinary in the sense of "in addition to" the ordinary (as well as being outstanding and exceptional!). Ordinary ministers of Holy Communion are the ordained and those properly installed as acolytes, usually seminarians. In parishes today there are simply not enough "ordinary" ministers of Holy Communion, so we call forth additional ministers, referred to as "extraordinary." Imagine how long the distribution of Communion would take if only the ordained or seminarians were those who distributed! It is not only because of need, however, that we have extraordinary ministers of Holy Communion. It is also by virtue of one's baptism. We parishioners are grateful that so many baptized Christians respond to the call to serve as extraordinary ministers of Holy Communion. In so doing we are reminded that we are all holy, and we are all called to ministry by virtue of our Christian baptism.

Preparing for This Ministry

Though different dioceses and parishes have slightly different preparation requirements for those who would be extraordinary ministers of Holy Communion, there is preparation nonetheless. We hope that this book will be a source of reflection for such preparation, and also for ongoing reflection throughout one's ministry. We know that it is not enough to simply attend a training event and never look back. Each ministry of the church requires regular prayer, reflection, reading, and thoughtfulness. This book is intended to assist with that process by providing prayers and reflection for each Sunday and for certain solemnities. This resource can also be used by groups who would like to share their faith with questions that prompt discussion.

Holy Communion for the Homebound and Sick

In the New Testament Letter of James we learn about the concern and care that the early Christians had for those members of their community who were sick. Such care and concern was a hallmark of Jesus's own ministry, and it has been a Christian charism ever since. Each week there are parishioners who are not able to join us for the liturgy, and so the Eucharist is brought to them as a sign of our unity. Extraordinary ministers of Holy Communion are often those who perform this ministry, and, in so doing, they extend the parish's reach to so many more fellow parishioners. This book is intended to be a resource for them as well.

Adapting This Resource for Holy Communion for the Homebound and Sick

The ritual text for use by extraordinary ministers (The Ordinary Rite of Communion of the Sick, from Administration of Communion and Viaticum to the Sick by an Extraordinary Minister) is provided as a separate publication to this book and enclosed within. Those who are extraordinary ministers of Holy Communion have undoubtedly been made familiar with this rite as part of their preparation. This book may be adapted for use with the rite, by sharing the gospel reflection, the prayers, or even the reflection question, so that the visit becomes a true ministry. It is to be remembered that ministers are not mere functionaries. As such, extraordinary ministers of Holy Communion bring not only the presence of Christ in the eucharistic species, but the presence of Christ in their very person by virtue of their baptism. So this book has been designed with that in mind, and it can be used to assist with making this a meaningful encounter and ministry.

The gospel today calls us to be vigilant, not afraid. Preparing our hearts for the coming of Christ, we call to mind our need for his mercy . . .

Prayer

O God who created the sun, the moon, and the stars, long ago you promised to redeem your people Israel, and that oath was fulfilled in Christ's coming among us. Help us to grow in love, humility, and justice as we patiently await the day when the Son of Man returns in glory. We ask this through Christ, our Lord. **Amen.**

Gospel **Luke 21:25-28, 34-36**

Jesus said to his disciples: "There will be signs in the sun, the moon, and the stars, and on earth nations will be in dismay, perplexed by the roaring of the sea and the waves. People will die of fright in anticipation of what is coming upon the world, for the powers of the heavens will be shaken. And then they will see the Son of Man coming in a cloud with power and great glory. But when these signs begin to happen, stand erect and raise your heads because your redemption is at hand.

"Beware that your hearts do not become drowsy from carousing and drunkenness and the anxieties of daily life, and that day catch you by surprise like a trap. For that day will assault everyone who lives on the face of the earth. Be vigilant at all times and pray that you have the strength to escape the tribulations that are imminent and to stand before the Son of Man."

Brief Silence

For Reflection

In today's first reading, Jeremiah addresses exiles who have experienced disaster after disaster, and who are grasping for some sign of hope. "The days are coming" is an expression that in the Bible ordinarily introduces a pronouncement of judgment, instilling fear in the hearers. Instead, Jeremiah uses the phrase to startle the careworn exiles with an assurance that God will fulfill the promises made to Israel and Judah.

While Jeremiah's hearers were waiting for fulfillment of God's promises in an existing crisis, Luke's hearers are waiting for an apocalyptic end time that seems long in coming. Luke's warning in today's gospel is not to let one's heart grow drowsy during the long wait. Like lovers whose passion fades and whose lives are lulled into routine, the people's ardor may dim and they may become unprepared for the coming crisis. Luke advises not letting our hearts go after things that satisfy only for a time, and not becoming weighed down with anxiety. Be always watchful, he says. Pray for strength, and do not be afraid. Stand tall, he says, raise your heads, and be ready for the embrace of the One who is Love Incarnate.

✦ How could you "lift your soul" to God this week? How might you carve out a little space of stillness so that you can listen to God's loving voice?

Brief Silence

Prayer

The psalmist writes, "You open wide your hand and satisfy the desire of every living thing" (Ps 145:16). Loving God, give us grateful hearts to receive the gifts you share, trusting you provide us with all we need. In a special way, open our hearts to the gift of yourself in this Eucharist so that we might know you more fully, love you more deeply, and serve you more faithfully in all we do. **Amen.**

Our psalm today reminds us of the great things that God has done for us and invites us to be filled with joy. Preparing ourselves for the joy God promises, let us call to mind the times we have failed to love our God and our neighbor . . .

Prayer

Lord Jesus, before you walked the earth in human form, the prophets foretold your coming, and John the Baptist proclaimed that the time was close at hand. May we now be faithful partners in spreading your gospel of love to a world very much in need of your good news. In your holy name we pray. **Amen**.

Gospel **Luke 3:1-6**

In the fifteenth year of the reign of Tiberius Caesar, when Pontius Pilate was governor of Judea, and Herod was tetrarch of Galilee, and his brother Philip tetrarch of the region of Ituraea and Trachonitis, and Lysanias was tetrarch of Abilene, during the high priesthood of Annas and Caiaphas, the word of God came to John the son of Zechariah in the desert. John went throughout the whole region of the Jordan, proclaiming a baptism of repentance for the forgiveness of sins, as it is written in the book of the words of the prophet Isaiah: / *A voice of one crying out in the desert: / "Prepare the way of the Lord, / make straight his paths. / Every valley shall be filled / and every mountain and hill shall be made low. / The winding roads shall be made straight, / and the rough ways made smooth, / and all flesh shall see the salvation of God."*

Brief Silence

For Reflection

In today's gospel, the narrative starts on an ominous note, as the ministry of John the Baptist is set against the backdrop of the Roman imperial rulers. Luke is not simply displaying an interest in history. He is reminding his hearers of the omnipresent imperial power that kept the inhabitants of Palestine in fear and grief. He foreshadows the terror of John's execution and of Jesus's crucifixion by introducing Herod and Pilate before these two prophets have even spoken their opening words.

It is in this context that we hear John's invitation to turn away from personal choices that impede God's coming and turn toward divine mercy. Using Isaiah's words, John first speaks in imperatives: prepare and make straight the way. But then the verbs shift to the passive voice, implying that it will be the Coming One himself who will fill in the valleys and level the mountains, straighten out winding roads and smooth the rough ways.

For them and for us, his coming does not eliminate these challenges along life's path but fills us with saving joy, justice, forgiveness, and mercy as we open ourselves to the great things God has done and continues to do for us.

✦ What does your baptism mean to you in this season of life? If you don't know the date, try to find out and add it to your calendar for the coming year. How could you remember or honor that date in a special way?

Brief Silence

Prayer

The psalmist writes, "You open wide your hand and satisfy the desire of every living thing" (Ps 145:16). Loving God, give us grateful hearts to receive the gifts you share, trusting you provide us with all we need. In a special way, open our hearts to the gift of yourself in this Eucharist so that we might know you more fully, love you more deeply, and serve you more faithfully in all we do. **Amen.**

THE IMMACULATE CONCEPTION OF THE BLESSED VIRGIN MARY

The Lord has made his salvation known in the sight of all the nations. Coming before the Lord, we ask for his pardon and peace . . .

Prayer

God of grace, you created the Blessed Virgin Mary to play a pivotal role in the redemption of the world. Like her, we want to believe that nothing is impossible with you: help us to grow in trust, that we might have the courage to sing of your wondrous deeds and to say "your will be done." With Mary and all the saints, we pray. **Amen**.

Gospel **Luke 1:26-38**

The angel Gabriel was sent from God to a town of Galilee called Nazareth, to a virgin betrothed to a man named Joseph, of the house of David, and the virgin's name was Mary. And coming to her, he said, "Hail, full of grace! The Lord is with you." But she was greatly troubled at what was said and pondered what sort of greeting this might be. Then the angel said to her, "Do not be afraid, Mary, for you have found favor with God. Behold, you will conceive in your womb and bear a son, and you shall name him Jesus. He will be great and will be called Son of the Most High, and the Lord God will give him the throne of David his father, and he will rule over the house of Jacob forever, and of his Kingdom there will be no end." But Mary said to the angel, "How can this be, since I have no relations with a man?" And the angel said to her in reply, "The Holy Spirit will come upon you, and the power of the Most High will overshadow you. Therefore the child to be born will be called holy, the Son of God. And behold, Elizabeth, your relative, has also conceived a son in her old age, and this is the sixth month for her who was called barren; for nothing will be impossible for God." Mary said, "Behold, I am the handmaid of the Lord. May it be done to me according to your word." Then the angel departed from her.

Brief Silence

For Reflection

Since this passage from Luke's Gospel recounts the surprise visit of the angel Gabriel to Mary, we might get the impression that the immaculate conception concerns the incarnation of Jesus within Mary's womb. Yes—but indirectly. While this solemnity celebrates Mary's freedom from original sin, most things in the Catholic tradition ultimately point us to Jesus.

When Mary is asked to be the mother of our Lord and says, "May it be done to me according to your word," she is not weighed down by this same baggage of sin or by misguided desire. Not that Mary is unafraid of following God or even devoid of temptation to do otherwise—on the contrary, the Scriptures tell us that she is greatly troubled by the angel's greeting—but she can look this fear, doubt, uncertainty, and future hardship in the eye and give a wholehearted *yes* to God's plan for her and for each of us. God preserved Mary from the stain of original sin, not for her own sake primarily but for the salvation of the world. In granting Mary the grace of her immaculate conception, God prepares the world for Jesus.

✦ How might God be calling you to bear Jesus to the world?

Brief Silence

Prayer

The psalmist writes, "You open wide your hand and satisfy the desire of every living thing" (Ps 145:16). Loving God, give us grateful hearts to receive the gifts you share, trusting you provide us with all we need. In a special way, open our hearts to the gift of yourself in this Eucharist so that we might know you more fully, love you more deeply, and serve you more faithfully in all we do. **Amen.**

Today's reading from Revelation assures us that salvation and power have come in Christ. We turn to his saving power as we prepare our hearts to receive Christ more fully . . .

Prayer

God of all blessings, Saint Juan Diego was once gifted by a surprise visit from Our Lady, who addressed herself as his Mother. We ask you to grant us the grace and humility to be like Juan Diego and like Mary: open to the unexpected. In this way, may we welcome the stranger, seeing Christ in all those we encounter. In Jesus's name we pray. **Amen.**

Gospel **Luke 1:26-38 (or Luke 1:39-47)**

The angel Gabriel was sent from God to a town of Galilee called Nazareth, to a virgin betrothed to a man named Joseph, of the house of David, and the virgin's name was Mary. And coming to her, he said, "Hail, full of grace! The Lord is with you." But she was greatly troubled at what was said and pondered what sort of greeting this might be. Then the angel said to her, "Do not be afraid, Mary, for you have found favor with God. Behold, you will conceive in your womb and bear a son, and you shall name him Jesus. He will be great and will be called Son of the Most High, and the Lord God will give him the throne of David his father, and he will rule over the house of Jacob forever, and of his Kingdom there will be no end." But Mary said to the angel, "How can this be, since I have no relations with a man?" And the angel said to her in reply, "The Holy Spirit will come upon you, and the power of the Most High will overshadow you. Therefore the child to be born will be called holy, the Son of God. And behold, Elizabeth, your relative, has also conceived a son in her old age, and this is the sixth month for her who was called barren; for nothing will be impossible for God."

Mary said, "Behold, I am the handmaid of the Lord. May it be done to me according to your word." Then the angel departed from her.

Brief Silence

For Reflection

The words of Mary's Magnificat—"He has thrown down the rulers from their thrones / but lifted up the lowly" (Luke 1:52)—are very much at the heart of her message to Juan Diego in Guadalupe. God chooses the humble and the downcast as the central messengers of the gospel.

The celebration of Our Lady of Guadalupe is a powerful reminder of our need to center the decentered in our church, to invite those on the outside and to listen to voices oft-discarded. Mary affirmed the dignity of all people and fulfilled the words she spoke in the Magnificat, aiding God's promise to lift up the lowly. Through the faithful witness of Juan Diego, Mary brought the whole of Mexico to her Son and today stands as an important beacon of hope for Latin America. In this model, we also are called to share our hope in Christ with others, especially those who are downtrodden and on the margins of society, offering healing in mind, body, and soul. Those who are poor and lowly, like Juan Diego, most closely resemble the Christ crucified and risen whom we worship. By welcoming them, we welcome our Lord himself.

✦ Our Lady of Guadalupe reminds us that God stands with the poor and marginalized in a privileged way. How might you, as an individual, better stand in solidarity with those on the margins of society? How could your community offer support to communities in greater need?

Brief Silence

Prayer

The psalmist writes, "You open wide your hand and satisfy the desire of every living thing" (Ps 145:16). Loving God, give us grateful hearts to receive the gifts you share, trusting you provide us with all we need. In a special way, open our hearts to the gift of yourself in this Eucharist so that we might know you more fully, love you more deeply, and serve you more faithfully in all we do. **Amen.**

Today's psalm joyfully announces that the Holy One of Israel is among us. Confident in his mercy, let us turn to God, mindful of the times that we have strayed from his grace . . .

Prayer

God of expectation, to you we cry out with joy and gladness, trusting that you are always in our midst. Let us heed the words of John the Baptist to share with others the gifts we have been given. In doing so, we pray to know your everlasting peace. In Jesus's name we pray. **Amen**.

Gospel **Luke 3:10-18**

The crowds asked John the Baptist, "What should we do?" He said to them in reply, "Whoever has two cloaks should share with the person who has none. And whoever has food should do likewise." Even tax collectors came to be baptized and they said to him, "Teacher, what should we do?" He answered them, "Stop collecting more than what is prescribed." Soldiers also asked him, "And what is it that we should do?" He told them, "Do not practice extortion, do not falsely accuse anyone, and be satisfied with your wages."

Now the people were filled with expectation, and all were asking in their hearts whether John might be the Christ. John answered them all, saying, "I am baptizing you with water, but one mightier than I is coming. I am not worthy to loosen the thongs of his sandals. He will baptize you with the Holy Spirit and fire. His winnowing fan is in his hand to clear his threshing floor and to gather the wheat into his barn, but the chaff he will burn with unquenchable fire." Exhorting them in many other ways, he preached good news to the people.

Brief Silence

For Reflection

The theme of joy weaves throughout the readings and the liturgy on this Gaudete (Latin for "rejoice") Sunday. The joy is not only ours; God too rejoices and sings, delighting in renewing us in love (Zeph 3:17-18). This joy and mutual delight want to be shared in wider and wider circles.

In the gospel John the Baptist speaks about a more advanced stage of turning toward God. Beyond the baptism of repentance and its freeing joy is a further "baptism" with "the Holy Spirit and fire" that the Christ brings. Followers of Jesus will undergo a purification process, a winnowing away of any imperfections that impede God's love and joy. The winnowing is not so much a process that separates good people from sinful ones; rather, it is a refining for all who turn to Christ, a burning away of all that keeps us from experiencing God's delight and from knowing how to share that with others. This, then, is what distinguishes joy from optimism. A cheery outlook is not necessarily a Christian virtue. But a radical joy that accompanies a refinement by fire is one of the paradoxical hallmarks of our faith.

✦ The first and second readings both tell us to rejoice, but life does not always lend itself to rejoicing. How do you find the joy God promises in the midst of life's darker seasons?

Brief Silence

Prayer

The psalmist writes, "You open wide your hand and satisfy the desire of every living thing" (Ps 145:16). Loving God, give us grateful hearts to receive the gifts you share, trusting you provide us with all we need. In a special way, open our hearts to the gift of yourself in this Eucharist so that we might know you more fully, love you more deeply, and serve you more faithfully in all we do. **Amen.**

Today's reading from Micah assures us that the Messiah is peace. Confident that Christ wishes to bring us the peace of his healing, we seek his pardon for those times when we have strayed from him . . .

Prayer

Lord Jesus, in these final days before we commemorate your birth, we are keenly aware of the need for your presence in our world. As Elizabeth recognized you in your mother's womb, may we recognize you in every person we meet. We turn to you, trusting in your salvation. Come, O come, Emmanuel! **Amen**.

Gospel **Luke 1:39-45**

Mary set out and traveled to the hill country in haste to a town of Judah, where she entered the house of Zechariah and greeted Elizabeth. When Elizabeth heard Mary's greeting, the infant leaped in her womb, and Elizabeth, filled with the Holy Spirit, cried out in a loud voice and said, "Blessed are you among women, and blessed is the fruit of your womb. And how does this happen to me, that the mother of my Lord should come to me? For at the moment the sound of your greeting reached my ears, the infant in my womb leaped for joy. Blessed are you who believed that what was spoken to you by the Lord would be fulfilled."

Brief Silence

For Reflection

In a culture in which a woman was esteemed for the male children she bore, Elizabeth likely endured accusatory glances and unkind comments throughout her life as people wondered why God was punishing her with barrenness. Likewise, in Mary's little village, Nazareth, the gossip about her probably started flying once her condition was known. Elizabeth, who has been utterly faithful to God all her life long (Luke 1:6), despite the suffering she has endured, is the perfect companion for Mary. She helps Mary learn to trust even more deeply the mysterious ways of God, as she endures the many difficulties that come with saying yes to God.

In like manner, we too carry the mysterious power of God's life within us, which enables us to be a source of delight and blessing for others. When we abandon ourselves to the mysterious ways of God, it is not only for ourselves that the new life within is given. We are meant to be companions to one another, a source of mutual joy, wisdom, and strength.

✦ Elizabeth recognizes something holy in what she could have experienced as ordinary fetal movement. Where have you found God in the everyday experiences of your life?

Brief Silence

Prayer

The psalmist writes, "You open wide your hand and satisfy the desire of every living thing" (Ps 145:16). Loving God, give us grateful hearts to receive the gifts you share, trusting you provide us with all we need. In a special way, open our hearts to the gift of yourself in this Eucharist so that we might know you more fully, love you more deeply, and serve you more faithfully in all we do. **Amen.**

Today is born our Savior, Christ the Lord. With the humility to which we are called by Christ's coming into the world to dwell among us, we ask for forgiveness and mercy . . .

Prayer

Prince of Peace, by your birth the world was made whole, and through your light the darkness was overcome. Let us, like the shepherds, be reminded that we need not be afraid, for today is born our Savior, Christ the Lord! May we go now to proclaim this good news. **Amen.**

Gospel **Luke 2:1-14; Mass during the Night**

In those days a decree went out from Caesar Augustus that the whole world should be enrolled. This was the first enrollment, when Quirinius was governor of Syria. So all went to be enrolled, each to his own town. And Joseph too went up from Galilee from the town of Nazareth to Judea, to the city of David that is called Bethlehem, because he was of the house and family of David, to be enrolled with Mary, his betrothed, who was with child. While they were there, the time came for her to have her child, and she gave birth to her firstborn son. She wrapped him in swaddling clothes and laid him in a manger, because there was no room for them in the inn.

Now there were shepherds in that region living in the fields and keeping the night watch over their flock. The angel of the Lord appeared to them and the glory of the Lord shone around them, and they were struck with great fear. The angel said to them, "Do not be afraid; for behold, I proclaim to you good news of great joy that will be for all the people. For today in the city of David a savior has been born for you who is Christ and Lord. And this will be a sign for you: you will find an infant wrapped in swaddling clothes and lying in a manger." And suddenly there was a multitude of the heavenly host with the angel, praising God and saying: / "Glory to God in the highest / and on earth peace to those on whom his favor rests."

Brief Silence

For Reflection

Today's gospel reading describes the conditions under which God enters the world as man: to a family in Bethlehem, in the region of Judea, while Caesar Augustus ruled the Roman Empire. The birth of Jesus to Mary is something *historical.* God takes on a human nature, in a certain time and place, under a particular set of circumstances.

Importantly, it is not through worldly leaders that God enters the world; they have received their reward. Whereas Emperor Augustus rules with pomp and circumstance, Jesus, Son of God, though born of the line of David, is born to a poor Galilean family for whom there is not even a place to stay in the inn. The light of Christ shines brightest precisely because of his lack of worldly status. In his lowliness, Jesus stands infinitely above all earthly powers. God enters the world with no stature, no fame, and no honor, nothing to conceal all that is given in Christ—that is, the infinite and personal love of God for you and for me. That light is enough to reach even the darkest parts of our own hearts, inviting us into the peace that Christ comes to bring.

✦ How is your heart this Christmas? Are you able to enter into the joy of the season, or is this year a challenge? How might your community support you where you are struggling?

Brief Silence

Prayer

The psalmist writes, "You open wide your hand and satisfy the desire of every living thing" (Ps 145:16). Loving God, give us grateful hearts to receive the gifts you share, trusting you provide us with all we need. In a special way, open our hearts to the gift of yourself in this Eucharist so that we might know you more fully, love you more deeply, and serve you more faithfully in all we do. **Amen.**

THE HOLY FAMILY OF JESUS, MARY, AND JOSEPH

The Holy Family is a living symbol of God's Providence and protection in the midst of sin. For those times that we have strayed from God, let us return to his providential mercy . . .

Prayer

God of love, you give us the example of the Holy Family that we may better love the people around us. We pray for the steady presence of Joseph, the grace of our Mother, Mary, and the wisdom of your Son, Jesus. May their witness encourage and guide us in our everyday lives. We ask this through Christ, our Lord. **Amen.**

Gospel **Luke 2:41-52**

Each year Jesus' parents went to Jerusalem for the feast of Passover, and when he was twelve years old, they went up according to festival custom. After they had completed its days, as they were returning, the boy Jesus remained behind in Jerusalem, but his parents did not know it. Thinking that he was in the caravan, they journeyed for a day and looked for him among their relatives and acquaintances, but not finding him, they returned to Jerusalem to look for him. After three days they found him in the temple, sitting in the midst of the teachers, listening to them and asking them questions, and all who heard him were astounded at his understanding and his answers. When his parents saw him, they were astonished, and his mother said to him, "Son, why have you done this to us? Your father and I have been looking for you with great anxiety." And he said to them, "Why were you looking for me? Did you not know that I must be in my Father's house?" But they did not understand what he said to them. He went down with them and came to Nazareth, and was obedient to them; and his mother kept all these things in her heart. And Jesus advanced in wisdom and age and favor before God and man.

Brief Silence

For Reflection

Luke portrays Jesus's earthly parents as loving followers of God's law and God's will. Mary assents to Gabriel, though she doesn't understand all that it entails. Mary and Joseph have their child circumcised after eight days and then present him in the Jerusalem temple, as the law prescribes. Every year, they go to Jerusalem for Passover. We might see, then, in the ending of today's gospel, that there is no conflict between Jesus's obedience to Mary and Joseph and his obedience to the will of God. Rather, it is Mary and Joseph who have taught Jesus how to recognize God's call and obey it. It is in their home in Nazareth that he will grow in wisdom and grace and come to understand how precious and beloved he is as God's Chosen One. It is from listening to his mother's song, which dreams of the hungry being well fed and the lowly lifted up, that Jesus learns obedience to God's inclusive love. We too learn in our homes that we are already God's beloved children, as the reading from 1 John asserts; it is not a privilege to be earned but a gift already bestowed.

✦ In this week's readings, Jesus and Samuel both show us the importance of sacred space. What places have been meaningful in your walk with God? Where do you find God most clearly present?

Brief Silence

Prayer

The psalmist writes, "You open wide your hand and satisfy the desire of every living thing" (Ps 145:16). Loving God, give us grateful hearts to receive the gifts you share, trusting you provide us with all we need. In a special way, open our hearts to the gift of yourself in this Eucharist so that we might know you more fully, love you more deeply, and serve you more faithfully in all we do. **Amen.**

SOLEMNITY OF MARY, THE HOLY MOTHER OF GOD

Mary teaches us to ponder God's wondrous mercy without ceasing. Let us turn to God as we ask for God's pardon and peace . . .

Prayer

O God of surprises, like the shepherds, we are amazed at the message of your Son, Jesus. Like them, may we also praise you. And like the Virgin Mary, may we have the grace and wisdom to ponder the mysteries of your love, day after day. In Jesus's name we pray. **Amen**.

Gospel **Luke 2:16-21**

The shepherds went in haste to Bethlehem and found Mary and Joseph, and the infant lying in the manger. When they saw this, they made known the message that had been told them about this child. All who heard it were amazed by what had been told them by the shepherds. And Mary kept all these things, reflecting on them in her heart. Then the shepherds returned, glorifying and praising God for all they had heard and seen, just as it had been told to them.

When eight days were completed for his circumcision, he was named Jesus, the name given him by the angel before he was conceived in the womb.

Brief Silence

For Reflection

In the Bible, bestowing a name is a critically important act. Naming is a way of identifying relationship, as the first human does when God presents the animals to him to see what he will call them (Gen 2:19). Often a name reflects something of the nature of the person, as when Adam calls the first woman "Eve, because she was the mother of all the living" (Gen 3:20, NABRE). Sometimes the name expresses the parents' experience of God, as when Hannah names her son Samuel, explaining, "I have asked him of the LORD" (1 Sam 1:20, NRSV). Just so, Elizabeth and Zechariah name their son "John," "God is gracious," or "gift of God," since they know it is not by human means alone that this child was conceived. Mary and Joseph call their son Jesus, whose name evokes the Hebrew expression "God saves" (see Matt 1:21), expressing their longing for a new experience of God's freeing power for themselves and their people from all that holds them bound.
On this day when we pray for world peace, the readings invite Jesus's followers to claim our inheritance from the One after whom we are named.

✦ What hopes and fears do you bring to this new year? How might you invite God into them?

Brief Silence

Prayer

The psalmist writes, "You open wide your hand and satisfy the desire of every living thing" (Ps 145:16). Loving God, give us grateful hearts to receive the gifts you share, trusting you provide us with all we need. In a special way, open our hearts to the gift of yourself in this Eucharist so that we might know you more fully, love you more deeply, and serve you more faithfully in all we do. **Amen.**

The light of Christ has dispelled the darkness that covered the earth. Coming before him, we ask him to fill our hearts with his light as we ask for his mercy and peace . . .

Prayer

Lord Jesus, the magi traveled from afar to pay you homage: we need only look within our hearts to recognize that we owe you our very lives, and to see that we ought to follow in the steps of those wise ones. May every nation on earth indeed adore you! In your holy name we pray. **Amen**.

Gospel **Matt 2:1-12**

When Jesus was born in Bethlehem of Judea, in the days of King Herod, behold, magi from the east arrived in Jerusalem, saying, "Where is the newborn king of the Jews? We saw his star at its rising and have come to do him homage." When King Herod heard this, he was greatly troubled, and all Jerusalem with him. Assembling all the chief priests and the scribes of the people, he inquired of them where the Christ was to be born. They said to him, "In Bethlehem of Judea, for thus it has been written through the prophet: / *And you, Bethlehem, land of Judah, / are by no means least among the rulers of Judah; / since from you shall come a ruler, / who is to shepherd my people Israel.*" / Then Herod called the magi secretly and ascertained from them the time of the star's appearance. He sent them to Bethlehem and said, "Go and search diligently for the child. When you have found him, bring me word, that I too may go and do him homage." After their audience with the king they set out. And behold, the star that they had seen at its rising preceded them, until it came and stopped over the place where the child was. They were overjoyed at seeing the star, and on entering the house they saw the child with Mary his mother.

They prostrated themselves and did him homage. Then they opened their treasures and offered him gifts of gold, frankincense, and myrrh. And having been warned in a dream not to return to Herod, they departed for their country by another way.

Brief Silence

For Reflection

There is a Hispanic tradition that on *El Día de los Reyes*, the "Day of the Kings," a small plastic baby Jesus is hidden in a cake, signifying the efforts to hide the child Jesus from the evil intentions of King Herod. As the cake is cut, the slicing knife represents the danger posed to Jesus by the cruel king. In some places, whoever finds the baby Jesus in his or her portion receives gifts. These traditions make tangible both the danger and the joy of Christ's coming.

In the gospel, the danger is most palpable as the visitors from the East wisely discern the true king who has been revealed, in contrast to Rome's puppet king, who wants to end the child's life. But a divine warning in a dream directs the magi to return to their country by another way.

These visitors from an unknown land prompt us to reflect on the gifts that come to us in hidden ways from foreigners and strangers. Those who are different are often a source of fear for us, but in today's gospel, they are friends, coheirs to the promise, and the first to recognize the hidden plans of God.

✦ What twists and turns have you faced in your journey with God? Where has a dead end led to an unexpected revelation?

Brief Silence

Prayer

The psalmist writes, "You open wide your hand and satisfy the desire of every living thing" (Ps 145:16). Loving God, give us grateful hearts to receive the gifts you share, trusting you provide us with all we need. In a special way, open our hearts to the gift of yourself in this Eucharist so that we might know you more fully, love you more deeply, and serve you more faithfully in all we do. **Amen.**

Today we hear the Father's voice from heaven saying, "You are my beloved Son." Calling to mind the times we have not lived as God's beloved sons and daughters, we ask for his pardon and peace . . .

Prayer

God of rebirth and renewal, through the waters of our baptism, you cleansed our souls. May we always remember that, while we do not merit it, you love us as your daughters and sons, gathering us as your lambs and feeding us in due time. O bless the Lord, my soul! **Amen**.

Gospel **Luke 3:15-16, 21-22**

The people were filled with expectation, and all were asking in their hearts whether John might be the Christ. John answered them all, saying, "I am baptizing you with water, but one mightier than I is coming. I am not worthy to loosen the thongs of his sandals. He will baptize you with the Holy Spirit and fire."

After all the people had been baptized and Jesus also had been baptized and was praying, heaven was opened and the Holy Spirit descended upon him in bodily form like a dove. And a voice came from heaven, "You are my beloved Son; with you I am well pleased."

Brief Silence

For Reflection

In today's gospel reading, a heavenly revelation highlights Jesus's specialness as God's beloved. While the divine voice that came from heaven at Jesus's baptism is directed to him ("You are my beloved Son; with you I am well pleased"), it is worth noticing that Luke tells the story so that "all the people" who had been just baptized along with Jesus by John the Baptist are present on the scene. In this way, Luke hints that they, too, experience the delight of God in them, as they are washed clean, newly born, and favored.

As we recall our own baptism, we know that we too have been in that thin space where "heaven was opened" and the barrier between humanity and divinity is dissolved. With Jesus taking on human flesh, and then inviting us to partake of his flesh and blood, the special place he holds in God's affection is extended to all.

That God is partial to each of us is something startling. This divine favor causes wonder and also carries with it a mission.

✦ What does your baptismal identity mean to you? How do you live out the vows that you made (or your parents made on your behalf) at your baptism?

Brief Silence

Prayer

The psalmist writes, "You open wide your hand and satisfy the desire of every living thing" (Ps 145:16). Loving God, give us grateful hearts to receive the gifts you share, trusting you provide us with all we need. In a special way, open our hearts to the gift of yourself in this Eucharist so that we might know you more fully, love you more deeply, and serve you more faithfully in all we do. **Amen.**

In our gospel today, Jesus performs the first of his miracles and his disciples begin to believe in him. Calling to mind the times we have failed to follow Christ's gospel, we ask for his mercy . . .

Prayer

God of all miracles, how can we ever be silent when we marvel at your amazing works?! Upon each of us you have bestowed great gifts: may we be good stewards of all you have given us. We sing to you; we bless you; we proclaim your deeds to all the earth! Glorifying your name, we pray. **Amen**.

Gospel **John 2:1-11**

There was a wedding at Cana in Galilee, and the mother of Jesus was there. Jesus and his disciples were also invited to the wedding. When the wine ran short, the mother of Jesus said to him, "They have no wine." And Jesus said to her, "Woman, how does your concern affect me? My hour has not yet come." His mother said to the servers, "Do whatever he tells you." Now there were six stone water jars there for Jewish ceremonial washings, each holding twenty to thirty gallons. Jesus told them, "Fill the jars with water." So they filled them to the brim. Then he told them, "Draw some out now and take it to the headwaiter." So they took it. And when the headwaiter tasted the water that had become wine, without knowing where it came from—although the servers who had drawn the water knew—, the headwaiter called the bridegroom and said to him, "Everyone serves good wine first, and then when people have drunk freely, an inferior one; but you have kept the good wine until now." Jesus did this as the beginning of his signs at Cana in Galilee and so revealed his glory, and his disciples began to believe in him.

Brief Silence

For Reflection

The wedding scene in today's gospel depicts Jesus as hesitant to open his Spirit-given gifts in public. He thinks the time has not yet come. But, as his mother rightly discerns, the need is urgent. Like all prophets, Jesus is reluctant and objects, just as Jeremiah protested that he was too young, and Moses avowed that he could not speak well. Jesus's mother, however, seems to take on the role of the wedding planner. She works behind the scenes, using her gifts of insight and knowledge, setting the stage for the sign that Jesus will perform. She knows that the time has come for her Son to offer his gifts publicly to bring the marriage between humanity and divinity to consummation.

Just as a wedding is only the beginning of a lifelong love affair, so the sign Jesus performs at Cana is the beginning of his many signs that revealed his glory. It is also the beginning of the disciples' belief in Jesus, who himself is the bridegroom, as John the Baptist acknowledges (John 3:29). The gift of Jesus himself is one that far surpasses any other that we could have on our "wish list"!

✦ Think of a time when you have felt flooded by goodness. When has Jesus provided for you in a way that felt abundant?

Brief Silence

Prayer

The psalmist writes, "You open wide your hand and satisfy the desire of every living thing" (Ps 145:16). Loving God, give us grateful hearts to receive the gifts you share, trusting you provide us with all we need. In a special way, open our hearts to the gift of yourself in this Eucharist so that we might know you more fully, love you more deeply, and serve you more faithfully in all we do. **Amen.**

The words of the Lord are Spirit and life, bringing healing to our soul. Calling to mind our need for his mercy, we bring our hearts before the Lord . . .

Prayer

Your words, Lord, are spirit, and they are life. We ask for wisdom to understand more fully your words, your teaching, your will for our lives. Striving to follow the path before us, may we come to know what part we are meant to play in building the Body of Christ. Trusting in you, we pray. **Amen**.

Gospel **Luke 1:1-4; 4:14-21**

Since many have undertaken to compile a narrative of the events that have been fulfilled among us, just as those who were eyewitnesses from the beginning and ministers of the word have handed them down to us, I too have decided, after investigating everything accurately anew, to write it down in an orderly sequence for you, most excellent Theophilus, so that you may realize the certainty of the teachings you have received.

Jesus returned to Galilee in the power of the Spirit, and news of him spread throughout the whole region. He taught in their synagogues and was praised by all.

He came to Nazareth, where he had grown up, and went according to his custom into the synagogue on the sabbath day. He stood up to read and was handed a scroll of the prophet Isaiah. He unrolled the scroll and found the passage where it was written: */ The Spirit of the Lord is upon me, / because he has anointed me / to bring glad tidings to the poor. / He has sent me to proclaim liberty to captives / and recovery of sight to the blind, / to let the oppressed go free, / and to proclaim a year acceptable to the Lord. /*

Rolling up the scroll, he handed it back to the attendant and sat down, and the eyes of all in the synagogue looked intently at him. He said to them, "Today this Scripture passage is fulfilled in your hearing."

Brief Silence

For Reflection

In today's gospel, Jesus declares his mission in his hometown synagogue. He begins by saying that the power of the Holy Spirit is upon him. The Spirit is actually God's mission statement to the world, since prior to Jesus's coming, God's love in mission is first revealed by the Spirit's activity in creation. We can only know the "inside" mystery of God through the "outside" manifestation of the action and presence of the holy in the world and in human experience.

Scripture scholar Stephen Bevans has elaborated a missionary theology of the Spirit, naming it "God Inside Out." Today's gospel says that this Spirit now rests upon Jesus, who makes tangible the inner heart of God, who desires healing, wholeness, and jubilee justice. Luke says that "the eyes of all in the synagogue looked intently" at Jesus when he read from the prophet Isaiah. Could they see "God inside out" as he interpreted the Scripture passage as fulfilled in their hearing?

It is easy to imagine that as Jesus announced his embodiment of his divine mission, those who felt exiled in body or spirit heard a new promise of restoration and release, a new time of jubilation.

✦ Share a favorite Scripture passage. Why is it meaningful to you? What does it say to you about who God is?

Brief Silence

Prayer

The psalmist writes, "You open wide your hand and satisfy the desire of every living thing" (Ps 145:16). Loving God, give us grateful hearts to receive the gifts you share, trusting you provide us with all we need. In a special way, open our hearts to the gift of yourself in this Eucharist so that we might know you more fully, love you more deeply, and serve you more faithfully in all we do. **Amen.**

Today, Mary and Joseph bring the child Jesus to the temple, fulfilling the precepts of the law. Calling to mind how we have failed to fulfill God's law, we ask for his pardon and peace as we prepare to celebrate these sacred mysteries . . .

Prayer

Giver of all good gifts, although we know you fulfill your promises, we do not always recognize your presence among us. Like Simeon, may we wait patiently, trusting in your holy word. And like Anna, may we give thanks to you and speak of you to all who will listen. We ask this through Christ, our Lord. **Amen**.

Gospel **Luke 2:22-40**

When the days were completed for their purification according to the law of Moses, Mary and Joseph took Jesus up to Jerusalem to present him to the Lord, just as it is written in the law of the Lord, *Every male that opens the womb shall be consecrated to the Lord*, and to offer the sacrifice of *a pair of turtledoves or two young pigeons*, in accordance with the dictate in the law of the Lord.

Now there was a man in Jerusalem whose name was Simeon. This man was righteous and devout, awaiting the consolation of Israel, and the Holy Spirit was upon him. It had been revealed to him by the Holy Spirit that he should not see death before he had seen the Christ of the Lord. He came in the Spirit into the temple; and when the parents brought in the child Jesus to perform the custom of the law in regard to him, he took him into his arms and blessed God, saying: "Now, Master, you may let your servant go in peace, according to your word, for my eyes have seen your salvation, which you prepared in sight of all the peoples, a light for revelation to the Gentiles, and glory for your people Israel."

The child's father and mother were amazed at what was said about him; and Simeon blessed them and said to Mary his mother, "Behold, this child is destined for the fall and rise of many in Israel, and to be a sign that will be contradicted—and you yourself a sword will pierce—so that the thoughts of many hearts may be revealed." There was also a prophetess, Anna, the daughter of Phanuel, of the tribe of Asher. She was advanced in years, having lived seven years with her husband after her marriage, and then as a widow until she was eighty-four. She never left the temple, but worshiped night and day with fasting and prayer. And coming forward at that very time, she gave thanks to God and spoke about the child to all who were awaiting the redemption of Jerusalem.

When they had fulfilled all the prescriptions of the law of the Lord, they returned to Galilee, to their own town of Nazareth. The child grew and became strong, filled with wisdom; and the favor of God was upon him.

Brief Silence

For Reflection

The prophet Malachi promises that someday the Lord will return to the temple, with a messenger before him. In the gospel reading today, the Lord does return to the temple. Simeon, the temple priest, grasps the importance of this visit, first by recognizing that it is indeed the Lord whom he sees. Simeon has been waiting for the arrival of a savior, having been promised by God that he would be alive to witness it. God indeed appears, not in might or majesty but in the innocence of an infant.

Coming out of Advent, we might take this radical presence for granted—perhaps we have been admiring the nativity scene at our parish or in our home. Alternatively, we might expect God to appear in glory as "the Lord, mighty in battle," as today's psalm describes, picturing a God who appears decisively to solve all of our problems. When Christ reveals himself to us, whether in word, in sacrament, or in the face of another human being, will we recognize him? Or will we miss him because we are expecting something else?

✦ Simeon and Anna help Mary and Joseph begin to understand the unique role their child will play in salvation history. Who helps you hear God's call in your own life?

Brief Silence

Prayer

The psalmist writes, "You open wide your hand and satisfy the desire of every living thing" (Ps 145:16). Loving God, give us grateful hearts to receive the gifts you share, trusting you provide us with all we need. In a special way, open our hearts to the gift of yourself in this Eucharist so that we might know you more fully, love you more deeply, and serve you more faithfully in all we do. **Amen.**

The Lord alone is holy; he is the one who offers us strength and forgiveness for our sins. Let us turn to him as we ask for his pardon and peace . . .

Prayer

God of transformation, you called Simon Peter to follow you, despite his confession of being unworthy. And you have promised that when we turn to you, you will answer us. May we allow ourselves to be changed, that we can say with confidence, "send me!" In your name we pray. **Amen**.

Gospel **Luke 5:1-11**

While the crowd was pressing in on Jesus and listening to the word of God, he was standing by the Lake of Gennesaret. He saw two boats there alongside the lake; the fishermen had disembarked and were washing their nets. Getting into one of the boats, the one belonging to Simon, he asked him to put out a short distance from the shore. Then he sat down and taught the crowds from the boat. After he had finished speaking, he said to Simon, "Put out into deep water and lower your nets for a catch." Simon said in reply, "Master, we have worked hard all night and have caught nothing, but at your command I will lower the nets." When they had done this, they caught a great number of fish and their nets were tearing. They signaled to their partners in the other boat to come to help them. They came and filled both boats so that the boats were in danger of sinking. When Simon Peter saw this, he fell at the knees of Jesus and said, "Depart from me, Lord, for I am a sinful man." For astonishment at the catch of fish they had made seized him and all those with him, and likewise James and John, the sons of Zebedee, who were partners of Simon. Jesus said to Simon, "Do not be afraid; from now on you will be catching men." When they brought their boats to the shore, they left everything and followed him.

Brief Silence

For Reflection

It can happen anywhere, anytime, to anyone. For Isaiah, it was during a religious service in the temple, wrapped in incense and awe-inspiring ritual. For certain Galilean fishermen, it was when they were going about their normal, everyday lives, casting and catching, cleaning and communing. With Paul, it was when he was in an angry turmoil, dead set against the new movement of Jesus-followers, determined to keep them from ruining the tradition. The call to mission accompanied by God's transforming grace can strike at any moment.

What always happens when one experiences a call from God is that the immensity of the divine holiness is overpowering. In the face of God's unparalleled goodness, graciousness, and mercy, our own inadequacies and sinfulness loom all the larger. "Woe is me, I am doomed!" exclaims Isaiah. "Depart from me, Lord, for I am a sinful man," implores Peter. "I am . . . not fit to be called an apostle," insists Paul. God, however, is never deterred. The mission is never dependent upon the worthiness of the minister but upon God's grace. If people kept their focus on their own inabilities and shortcomings, the work of God would never be accomplished.

✦ Peter does not always live up to the reckless love with which he leaves everything and follows Jesus. His journey with Christ, like all of ours, will have ups and downs. Where are you on your walk with Jesus? How might Peter accompany you wherever you are?

Brief Silence

Prayer

The psalmist writes, "You open wide your hand and satisfy the desire of every living thing" (Ps 145:16). Loving God, give us grateful hearts to receive the gifts you share, trusting you provide us with all we need. In a special way, open our hearts to the gift of yourself in this Eucharist so that we might know you more fully, love you more deeply, and serve you more faithfully in all we do. **Amen.**

Jesus teaches us that those who are hungry will be filled and those who are weeping will one day laugh. Trusting in his mercy, we come before him seeking his peace . . .

Prayer

God of every blessing, the psalmist says those who hope in you are blessed, and Jesus told the crowds that many unfortunate situations are also a blessing in disguise. We trust not that we will be blessed at some later time, but that we are blessed now. May we meditate on this truth, now and always. Through Christ, our Lord. **Amen**.

Gospel **Luke 6:17, 20-26**

Jesus came down with the Twelve and stood on a stretch of level ground with a great crowd of his disciples and a large number of the people from all Judea and Jerusalem and the coastal region of Tyre and Sidon. And raising his eyes toward his disciples he said: / "Blessed are you who are poor, / for the kingdom of God is yours. / Blessed are you who are now hungry, / for you will be satisfied. / Blessed are you who are now weeping, / for you will laugh. / Blessed are you when people hate you, and when they exclude and insult you, and denounce your name as evil on account of the Son of Man. Rejoice and leap for joy on that day! Behold, your reward will be great in heaven. For their ancestors treated the prophets in the same way. / But woe to you who are rich, / for you have received your consolation. / Woe to you who are filled now, / for you will be hungry. / Woe to you who laugh now, / for you will grieve and weep. / Woe to you when all speak well of you, / for their ancestors treated the false prophets in this way."

Brief Silence

For Reflection

In biblical tradition, poverty is never an indicator of blessedness; it is always regarded as evil. What can Jesus mean by stating the opposite?

Whenever Jesus speaks about the poor, he addresses his words to disciples who are not among the most destitute. They have the means to be agents of divine blessing to those who are needy. His invitation to disciples is to embrace some form of being poor, but not destitution, as an essential aspect of their commitment to Jesus.

The blessedness that Jesus holds up is the happiness of those who are being liberated from their desperate poverty already in the here and now, a foretaste of the final elimination of all want in the fullness of the reign of God. It is not a wish for future reward, but a concrete possibility when the needs of real people are known and the resources are shared in community.

This could be a good time to renew our efforts at becoming agents of blessedness through our prayer for those who are in need, fasting in solidarity with those who are hungry not by choice, and almsgiving to those who are destitute.

✦ What suffering or lack in your life makes you doubt the presence of God? How could you come to find God present in that very thing?

Brief Silence

Prayer

The psalmist writes, "You open wide your hand and satisfy the desire of every living thing" (Ps 145:16). Loving God, give us grateful hearts to receive the gifts you share, trusting you provide us with all we need. In a special way, open our hearts to the gift of yourself in this Eucharist so that we might know you more fully, love you more deeply, and serve you more faithfully in all we do. **Amen.**

In our gospel today, Jesus calls us to forgive so that we will be forgiven and to stop judging so that we will not be judged. Recalling the times we have failed to follow Jesus's words, we remember our need for his mercy . . .

Prayer

Gracious God, we thank you for the love and mercy that you pour out so abundantly upon us. Thank you for your compassion, pardon, and redemption. May we hear and heed Jesus's words: help us to be less quick to judge and condemn and swifter to grant mercy and forgiveness to ourselves and others. In Jesus's name we pray. **Amen**.

Gospel **Luke 6:27-38**

Jesus said to his disciples: "To you who hear I say, love your enemies, do good to those who hate you, bless those who curse you, pray for those who mistreat you. To the person who strikes you on one cheek, offer the other one as well, and from the person who takes your cloak, do not withhold even your tunic. Give to everyone who asks of you, and from the one who takes what is yours do not demand it back. Do to others as you would have them do to you. For if you love those who love you, what credit is that to you? Even sinners love those who love them. And if you do good to those who do good to you, what credit is that to you? Even sinners do the same. If you lend money to those from whom you expect repayment, what credit is that to you? Even sinners lend to sinners, and get back the same amount. But rather, love your enemies and do good to them, and lend expecting nothing back; then your reward will be great and you will be children of the Most High, for he himself is kind to the ungrateful and the wicked. Be merciful, just as your Father is merciful.

"Stop judging and you will not be judged. Stop condemning and you will not be condemned. Forgive and you will be forgiven. Give, and gifts will be given to you; a good measure, packed together, shaken down, and overflowing, will be poured into your lap. For the measure with which you measure will in return be measured out to you."

Brief Silence

For Reflection

How is one to respond to the unearned gift of God's gracious mercy? The gospel gives the answer: by emulating the One whose child we are.

Jesus spells out some of the ways that God's children do as God does: loving enemies, doing good to those who do hateful things, blessing those who speak abusively, and praying for such people.

Beyond individual actions of non-retaliation, Jesus invites his followers into a fundamental stance in life that must be chosen so that we reflect the image of the One who made us. By opening ourselves to the immeasurable goodness, compassion, and love of the Most High, our puny capacities are stretched and expanded.

Such a life stance demands relinquishing what is our more natural reaction: to return in kind what we get. If someone strikes us, our instinct is to hit back. But Jesus points out that when evil is returned for evil, all it does is increase the measure of evil in the world.

What enables us to be compassionate, nonjudgmental, forgiving, and giving is that God has first been that way with us. Such divine action in us then shapes our ability to measure the way God does.

✦ Who do you perceive as your enemies? How could you expand your love for them? How could you extend radical forgiveness to someone who has hurt you?

Brief Silence

Prayer

The psalmist writes, "You open wide your hand and satisfy the desire of every living thing" (Ps 145:16). Loving God, give us grateful hearts to receive the gifts you share, trusting you provide us with all we need. In a special way, open our hearts to the gift of yourself in this Eucharist so that we might know you more fully, love you more deeply, and serve you more faithfully in all we do. **Amen.**

In our gospel today, Jesus asks us to recognize our own faults before we condemn and criticize those around us. Taking his words to heart, we call to mind our sins and ask for his pardon and peace . . .

Prayer

O God, you have created us to sing your praise and give you thanks! May our eyes perceive the goodness in others. May our mouths always speak with kindness and in truth. And may our hearts be fully devoted to you, that we might bear much fruit. We ask this through Christ, our Lord. **Amen**.

Gospel **Luke 6:39-45**

Jesus told his disciples a parable, "Can a blind person guide a blind person? Will not both fall into a pit? No disciple is superior to the teacher; but when fully trained, every disciple will be like his teacher. Why do you notice the splinter in your brother's eye, but do not perceive the wooden beam in your own? How can you say to your brother, 'Brother, let me remove that splinter in your eye,' when you do not even notice the wooden beam in your own eye? You hypocrite! Remove the wooden beam from your eye first; then you will see clearly to remove the splinter in your brother's eye.

"A good tree does not bear rotten fruit, nor does a rotten tree bear good fruit. For every tree is known by its own fruit. For people do not pick figs from thornbushes, nor do they gather grapes from brambles. A good person out of the store of goodness in his heart produces good, but an evil person out of a store of evil produces evil; for from the fullness of the heart the mouth speaks."

Brief Silence

For Reflection

The readings today prompt us to reflect on the care that is needed in speaking. In an age where public discourse, particularly during an election season, often degenerates into name-calling, false accusations, and impugning the character of others, a person of faith stands out by his or her refusal to speak ill of others. Moreover, the gospel warns that one who is blind to the goodness in others, and who speaks evil of them instead, reveals his or her own puny measure of openness to God's goodness. Those who see only their neighbors' tiny faults and rush to point those out expose the logjam that blocks their own hearts from receiving and giving God's unfathomable love. A starting point toward transformation of the heart that results in kind words can be vigilance over what one says, curbing the impulse to speak ill of another. That is only a beginning. The gospel envisions a point where the faithful disciple reaches maturity in cultivating inner goodness to such an extent that only good and kind speech would well up from within and pass through the lips.

✦ The image of being a thriving, fruit-bearing tree runs through the readings today. What fruits might God be calling you to bear?

Brief Silence

Prayer

The psalmist writes, "You open wide your hand and satisfy the desire of every living thing" (Ps 145:16). Loving God, give us grateful hearts to receive the gifts you share, trusting you provide us with all we need. In a special way, open our hearts to the gift of yourself in this Eucharist so that we might know you more fully, love you more deeply, and serve you more faithfully in all we do. **Amen.**

Today we begin this season of penitence to prepare ourselves for the paschal mystery of our Lord Jesus Christ. Let us begin by calling to mind our need to turn to him and to seek his mercy . . .

Prayer

Most merciful God, as we enter into this holy season of Lent, we hear your voice calling, "return to me." We acknowledge our sinful nature and our need for your grace and forgiveness. Cleanse our hearts and our minds, that we might become more like your Son, Jesus Christ, in whose holy name we pray. **Amen**.

Gospel **Matt 6:1-6, 16-18**

Jesus said to his disciples: "Take care not to perform righteous deeds in order that people may see them; otherwise, you will have no recompense from your heavenly Father. When you give alms, do not blow a trumpet before you, as the hypocrites do in the synagogues and in the streets to win the praise of others. Amen, I say to you, they have received their reward. But when you give alms, do not let your left hand know what your right is doing, so that your almsgiving may be secret. And your Father who sees in secret will repay you.

"When you pray, do not be like the hypocrites, who love to stand and pray in the synagogues and on street corners so that others may see them. Amen, I say to you, they have received their reward. But when you pray, go to your inner room, close the door, and pray to your Father in secret. And your Father who sees in secret will repay you.

"When you fast, do not look gloomy like the hypocrites. They neglect their appearance, so that they may appear to others to be fasting. Amen, I say to you, they have received their reward. But when you fast, anoint your head and wash your face, so that you may not appear to be fasting, except to your Father who is hidden. And your Father who sees what is hidden will repay you."

Brief Silence

For Reflection

Fasting helps us see more clearly the things that bring us closer to God while setting other things in their proper places. Who of us is not overly attached to *something*—financial success, social approval, political beliefs, workplace gossip—that gets in the way of right relationship with God and others? Are we willing to fast from these things? In today's gospel, by giving his prescriptions for fasting, Jesus asks us to put all things into perspective under the First Commandment: "I am the LORD your God." This Lent, are we willing to recognize Jesus as Lord of our whole lives, not just the parts we let him have?

When we fast, denying ourselves, we have more to give to God and to others—that's where prayer and almsgiving fit in, and Jesus addresses each in turn in the gospel reading. Both are gifts—gifts of our time and gifts of our treasure. Neither should be for selfish gain but should seek to praise, reverence, and serve, trusting that God will indeed "repay in secret." By "rending our hearts" this Lenten season, may we prepare to experience the love of God more fully at Easter.

✦ How can you make space this season for "your Father who sees in secret"? How might you carve out some silence and solitude in order to offer more of your heart to God?

Brief Silence

Prayer

The psalmist writes, "You open wide your hand and satisfy the desire of every living thing" (Ps 145:16). Loving God, give us grateful hearts to receive the gifts you share, trusting you provide us with all we need. In a special way, open our hearts to the gift of yourself in this Eucharist so that we might know you more fully, love you more deeply, and serve you more faithfully in all we do. **Amen.**

Our second reading from Saint Paul assures us that no one who believes in God will ever be put to shame. Confident in this promise, we approach God for those times that we have strayed from him . . .

Prayer

God of strength and consolation, we are often distracted by the trappings of this world; the allure of power and wealth can easily sway us. May we, like Jesus, resist the urge to go astray. And when we are tempted, we pray that you will be with us in times of trial. We ask this through Christ, our Lord. **Amen**.

Gospel **Luke 4:1-13**

Filled with the Holy Spirit, Jesus returned from the Jordan and was led by the Spirit into the desert for forty days, to be tempted by the devil. He ate nothing during those days, and when they were over he was hungry. The devil said to him, "If you are the Son of God, command this stone to become bread." Jesus answered him, "It is written, *One does not live on bread alone."* Then he took him up and showed him all the kingdoms of the world in a single instant. The devil said to him, "I shall give to you all this power and glory; for it has been handed over to me, and I may give it to whomever I wish. All this will be yours, if you worship me." Jesus said to him in reply, "It is written: *You shall worship the Lord, your God, and him alone shall you serve."* Then he led him to Jerusalem, made him stand on the parapet of the temple, and said to him, "If you are the Son of God, throw yourself down from here, for it is written: *He will command his angels concerning you, to guard you,* and: *With their hands they will support you, lest you dash your foot against a stone."* Jesus said to him in reply, "It also says, *You shall not put the Lord, your God, to the test."* When the devil had finished every temptation, he departed from him for a time.

Brief Silence

For Reflection

Where is God in the face of suffering—our own and that of so many millions of others? The readings today don't provide reasoned arguments in answer to these deep questions, but they do show us a way to engage the struggles as we are invited more deeply into the mystery of suffering, dying, and rising as God's cherished ones.

In the gospel, we see Jesus relying on the word of God to guide and strengthen him. He engages in a kind of Bible battle with the devil, a sobering reminder that anyone can quote Scripture to their own purposes. Jesus shows that daily immersion of ourselves in Scripture enables us to recognize the authentic voice of God and reject the traitorous lead of the tempter.

Lent provides us an opportunity to embrace anew such struggles as Jesus faced. Like him, we claim the power of the Spirit that has been given to us in baptism, and daily immerse ourselves in the word. Clarity in hearing that word comes when we go apart to deserted spaces, and when we fast so as to sharpen our hunger for God and for acting in solidarity with God's starving people.

✦ God's word plays a prominent role in this gospel. How do you pray with Scripture? How could you find ways to spend more time with it?

Brief Silence

Prayer

The psalmist writes, "You open wide your hand and satisfy the desire of every living thing" (Ps 145:16). Loving God, give us grateful hearts to receive the gifts you share, trusting you provide us with all we need. In a special way, open our hearts to the gift of yourself in this Eucharist so that we might know you more fully, love you more deeply, and serve you more faithfully in all we do. **Amen.**

Today's reading from Genesis reminds us of the blessings we receive when we wait upon God. For those times when we have lost patience and have strayed from him, we now seek his pardon and peace . . .

Prayer

You, Lord, are our light and our salvation; with you at our side, we have nothing to fear. As we ponder the story of the transfiguration this week, help us also to be transformed into more faithful disciples of Jesus. May we hope always in you, O God, in whose name we pray. **Amen**.

Gospel **Luke 9:28b-36**

Jesus took Peter, John, and James and went up the mountain to pray. While he was praying his face changed in appearance and his clothing became dazzling white. And behold, two men were conversing with him, Moses and Elijah, who appeared in glory and spoke of his exodus that he was going to accomplish in Jerusalem. Peter and his companions had been overcome by sleep, but becoming fully awake, they saw his glory and the two men standing with him. As they were about to part from him, Peter said to Jesus, "Master, it is good that we are here; let us make three tents, one for you, one for Moses, and one for Elijah." But he did not know what he was saying. While he was still speaking, a cloud came and cast a shadow over them, and they became frightened when they entered the cloud. Then from the cloud came a voice that said, "This is my chosen Son; listen to him." After the voice had spoken, Jesus was found alone. They fell silent and did not at that time tell anyone what they had seen.

Brief Silence

For Reflection

Luke's version of Jesus's transfiguration, which we hear every year on the Second Sunday of Lent, albeit from different gospels every year, offers unique details that the other gospels omit.

Luke alone notes that when Jesus goes up the mountain, his purpose is to pray. And only Luke tells us the topic of the conversation between Jesus, Moses, and Elijah: they "spoke of his exodus that he was going to accomplish in Jerusalem." Jesus is no fool. The handwriting is on the wall. Going to Jerusalem would be stoking the opposition to him that already existed there. As at every major turning point in the gospel, Jesus enters into deep communion with God as he discerns what to do.

During this intense prayer of discernment, Jesus is given sure signs that he is guided by God in his choice: the cloud of divine presence, the heavenly messengers, and his Father's own voice. Thus assured of God's love and direction, Jesus turns his transfigured face toward Jerusalem. Placing his own life in danger, Jesus makes a deliberate, prophetic choice to continue to "proclaim liberty to captives" (4:18), as he had declared in his hometown synagogue. His death is not an inevitable fate, but a choice for freeing love.

✦ The transfiguration reveals something about Jesus, but it also leaves the disciples bewildered and frightened. What is an area of your life that feels confusing or dark? How would you like God to shine God's light there?

Brief Silence

Prayer

The psalmist writes, "You open wide your hand and satisfy the desire of every living thing" (Ps 145:16). Loving God, give us grateful hearts to receive the gifts you share, trusting you provide us with all we need. In a special way, open our hearts to the gift of yourself in this Eucharist so that we might know you more fully, love you more deeply, and serve you more faithfully in all we do. **Amen.**

As Moses approached the presence of God in the burning bush, he bowed his head in humility, knowing that he walked on holy ground. As we prepare to come before the altar of the Lord, let us also come before him in humility, asking for his pardon and peace . . .

Prayer

God of kindness and mercy, throughout history, you have heard the cries of your people when they are suffering. We too are blessed by the pardon and healing you give to us. May we never cease to proclaim you as Lord and to make your name known. Trusting in you, we pray. **Amen**.

Gospel **Luke 13:1-9**

Some people told Jesus about the Galileans whose blood Pilate had mingled with the blood of their sacrifices. Jesus said to them in reply, "Do you think that because these Galileans suffered in this way they were greater sinners than all other Galileans? By no means! But I tell you, if you do not repent, you will all perish as they did! Or those eighteen people who were killed when the tower at Siloam fell on them—do you think they were more guilty than everyone else who lived in Jerusalem? By no means! But I tell you, if you do not repent, you will all perish as they did!"

And he told them this parable: "There once was a person who had a fig tree planted in his orchard, and when he came in search of fruit on it but found none, he said to the gardener, 'For three years now I have come in search of fruit on this fig tree but have found none. So cut it down. Why should it exhaust the soil?' He said to him in reply, 'Sir, leave it for this year also, and I shall cultivate the ground around it and fertilize it; it may bear fruit in the future. If not you can cut it down.' "

Brief Silence

For Reflection

A well-known evangelical preacher pointed a finger at the people of Haiti, declaring that their own sinfulness had brought down upon them the wrath of God in the form of an earthquake. It's such a simple explanation: if something bad happens, then the victims must have done something to deserve it. That's what Jesus figures people are thinking when they report to him about the people whom Pilate murdered and the people who were killed when a tower fell on them.

There may, indeed, be sinful causes behind these events, but not on the part of the victim. Pilate, who carries out violent execution of innocent people, embodies a sin-wracked system. Deaths caused by shoddy workmanship or construction shortcuts, when profit is prized over human safety, are the result of sinful practices, but not those of the ones who fall victim. In the gospel, Jesus does not answer the more complex question of why bad things happen to good people, but he does clearly dissociate untimely death from sin and guilt. What he emphasizes in his response is the need to always be prepared—the end could come quite unexpectedly. Are you ready?

✦ How might God be calling you to prune away some excess in this Lenten season so that you can bear greater fruit?

Brief Silence

Prayer

The psalmist writes, "You open wide your hand and satisfy the desire of every living thing" (Ps 145:16). Loving God, give us grateful hearts to receive the gifts you share, trusting you provide us with all we need. In a special way, open our hearts to the gift of yourself in this Eucharist so that we might know you more fully, love you more deeply, and serve you more faithfully in all we do. **Amen.**

In our gospel today, the Prodigal Son returns to his Father's house and there is much rejoicing. Remembering how much God desires us to come before him, we turn to him asking for his mercy . . .

Prayer

God of goodness, time and again you have provided for the needs of your people, even those who least deserve it. How frequently we rebel against you, and yet you continually care for us. May we be ever more aware of the gifts you have given us, that we may glorify your name. Together we pray. **Amen**.

Gospel **Luke 15:1-3, 11-32**

Tax collectors and sinners were all drawing near to listen to Jesus, but the Pharisees and scribes began to complain, saying, "This man welcomes sinners and eats with them." So to them Jesus addressed this parable: "A man had two sons, and the younger son said to his father, 'Father give me the share of your estate that should come to me.' So the father divided the property between them. After a few days, the younger son collected all his belongings and set off to a distant country where he squandered his inheritance on a life of dissipation. When he had freely spent everything, a severe famine struck that country, and he found himself in dire need. So he hired himself out to one of the local citizens who sent him to his farm to tend the swine. And he longed to eat his fill of the pods on which the swine fed, but nobody gave him any. Coming to his senses he thought, 'How many of my father's hired workers have more than enough food to eat, but here am I, dying from hunger. I shall get up and go to my father and I shall say to him, "Father, I have sinned against heaven and against you. I no longer deserve to be called your son; treat me as you would treat one of your hired workers.'" So he got up and went back to his father. While he was still a long way off, his father caught sight of him, and was filled with compassion. He ran to his son, embraced him and kissed him. His son said to him, 'Father, I have sinned against heaven and against you; I no longer deserve to be called your son.' But his father ordered his servants, 'Quickly bring the finest robe and put it on him; put a ring on his finger and sandals on his feet. Take the fattened calf and slaughter it. Then let us celebrate with a feast, because this son of mine was dead, and has come to life again; he was lost, and has been found.' Then the celebration began. Now the older son had been out in the field and, on his way back, as he neared the house, he heard the sound of music and dancing. He called one of the servants and asked what this might mean. The servant said to him, 'Your brother has returned and your father has slaughtered the fattened calf because he has him back safe and sound.' He became angry, and when he refused to enter the house, his father came out and pleaded with him. He said to his father in reply, 'Look, all these years I served you and not once did I disobey your orders; yet you never gave me even a young goat to feast on with my friends. But when your son returns who swallowed up your property with prostitutes, for him you slaughter the fattened calf.' He said to him, 'My son, you are here with me always; everything I have is yours. But now we must celebrate and rejoice, because your brother was dead and has come to life again; he was lost and has been found.'"

Brief Silence

For Reflection

What has brought the younger son in today's gospel parable back to life is not his own coming to his senses and his own efforts to return to the source of his heritage. Rather, it is the father's unfailing love, as he seeks him out and flings open his arms, wrapping him in a mantle of forgiveness, that resurrects in him the response of love and joy and gratitude, along with the sure knowledge that all is given freely and totally. This heritage cannot be earned, and it is never depleted, even by our most egregious misuses.

As a figure of the divine, the father offers a gift of reconciliation that shatters the too-narrow vision of children vying for a bigger piece of the pie, when all along the whole of the inheritance is offered to each and all, with no bounds. This gift begins a process of healing that expands our puny estimation of our inheritance and opens our capacity to be transformed by the Giver, enlarging our capacity to pass on that heritage to others.

✦ How do you experience God sustaining and nourishing you on your pilgrimage through this life? Where might God be providing abundance that you are overlooking?

Brief Silence

Prayer

The psalmist writes, "You open wide your hand and satisfy the desire of every living thing" (Ps 145:16). Loving God, give us grateful hearts to receive the gifts you share, trusting you provide us with all we need. In a special way, open our hearts to the gift of yourself in this Eucharist so that we might know you more fully, love you more deeply, and serve you more faithfully in all we do. **Amen.**

Jesus has mercy on us when we do not have mercy on ourselves. Calling to mind our constant need for his healing grace, we ask for his pardon and peace . . .

Prayer

God of forgiveness and love, you see our mistakes and our failings, and yet you remind us that our sins have already been forgiven. We ask that you continue to form us anew, so that we may persevere toward the goal of holiness, singing always of your mercy to us. We ask this through Christ, our Lord. **Amen**.

Gospel **John 8:1-11**

Jesus went to the Mount of Olives. But early in the morning he arrived again in the temple area, and all the people started coming to him, and he sat down and taught them. Then the scribes and the Pharisees brought a woman who had been caught in adultery and made her stand in the middle. They said to him, "Teacher, this woman was caught in the very act of committing adultery. Now in the law, Moses commanded us to stone such women. So what do you say?" They said this to test him, so that they could have some charge to bring against him. Jesus bent down and began to write on the ground with his finger. But when they continued asking him, he straightened up and said to them, "Let the one among you who is without sin be the first to throw a stone at her." Again he bent down and wrote on the ground. And in response, they went away one by one, beginning with the elders. So he was left alone with the woman before him. Then Jesus straightened up and said to her, "Woman, where are they? Has no one condemned you?" She replied, "No one, sir." Then Jesus said, "Neither do I condemn you. Go, and from now on do not sin any more."

Brief Silence

For Reflection

In today's gospel, Jesus encounters the woman caught in the act of committing adultery. Like Jesus's opponents in the gospel, Christian teachers and preachers have struggled to understand how Jesus could let a blatant sinner off without punishment. Saint Ambrose worried that the gospel could produce anxiety in the inexperienced and tried to dismiss the idea that Jesus could have made a mistake. John Calvin assured his followers that although Jesus remits our sins, he does not subvert the social order or abolish legal sentences and punishments.

While the latter may be true, Jesus does, indeed, abolish the notion that our relationship with God is contained within rules and law. While these are necessary for the peaceable ordering of any organization, whether civil or religious, law does not express adequately how God relates to us. It is God's freely given gift of forgiveness, offered to us in the person of Christ, that binds us to God and invites us to a new way of life. It is a gift that is replicated every time we offer forgiveness and compassion to one another.

✦ How could you grow in awareness of your own dependence on God? How might your life change if you truly understood that you are not in control?

Brief Silence

Prayer

The psalmist writes, "You open wide your hand and satisfy the desire of every living thing" (Ps 145:16). Loving God, give us grateful hearts to receive the gifts you share, trusting you provide us with all we need. In a special way, open our hearts to the gift of yourself in this Eucharist so that we might know you more fully, love you more deeply, and serve you more faithfully in all we do. **Amen.**

PALM SUNDAY OF THE LORD'S PASSION

Today we accompany the Lord Jesus as he enters into his passion. Preparing our hearts, we ask for his mercy . . .

Prayer

O God, as we recall the sacrifice Jesus made for us, we kneel before you and pray to know your help this day. As he emptied himself, may we give to others. As he was obedient, may we follow his example. And may we believe and profess that Jesus Christ is Lord, today and always. In your name we pray. **Amen**.

Gospel **Luke 23:1-49 (or Luke 22:14–23:56)**

The elders of the people, chief priests and scribes, arose and brought Jesus before Pilate. They brought charges against him, saying, "We found this man misleading our people; he opposes the payment of taxes to Caesar and maintains that he is the Christ, a king." Pilate asked him, "Are you the king of the Jews?" He said to him in reply, "You say so." Pilate then addressed the chief priests and the crowds, "I find this man not guilty." But they were adamant and said, "He is inciting the people with his teaching throughout all Judea, from Galilee where he began even to here."

On hearing this Pilate asked if the man was a Galilean; and upon learning that he was under Herod's jurisdiction, he sent him to Herod who was in Jerusalem at that time. Herod was very glad to see Jesus; he had been wanting to see him for a long time, for he had heard about him and had been hoping to see him perform some sign. He questioned him at length, but he gave him no answer. The chief priests and scribes, meanwhile, stood by accusing him harshly. Herod and his soldiers treated him contemptuously and mocked him, and after clothing him in resplendent garb, he sent him back to Pilate. Herod and Pilate became friends that very day, even though they had been enemies formerly. Pilate then summoned the chief priests, the rulers, and the people and said to them, "You brought this man to me and accused him of inciting the people to revolt. I have conducted my investigation in your presence and have not found this man guilty of the charges you have brought against him, nor did Herod, for he sent him back to us. So no capital crime has been committed by him. Therefore I shall have him flogged and then release him."

But all together they shouted out, "Away with this man! Release Barabbas to us."—Now Barabbas had been imprisoned for a rebellion that had taken place in the city and for murder.—Again Pilate addressed them, still wishing to release Jesus, but they continued their shouting, "Crucify him! Crucify him!" Pilate addressed them a third time, "What evil has this man done? I found him guilty of no capital crime. Therefore I shall have him flogged and then release him." With loud shouts, however, they persisted in calling for his crucifixion, and their voices prevailed. The verdict of Pilate was that their demand should be granted. So he released the man who had been imprisoned for rebellion and murder, for whom they asked, and he handed Jesus over to them to deal with as they wished.

As they led him away they took hold of a certain Simon, a Cyrenian, who was coming in from the country; and after laying the cross on him, they made him carry it behind Jesus. A large crowd of people followed Jesus, including many women who mourned and lamented him. Jesus turned to them and said, "Daughters of Jerusalem, do not weep for me; weep instead for yourselves and for your children for indeed, the days are coming when people will say, 'Blessed are the barren, the wombs that never bore and the breasts that never nursed.' At that time people will say to the mountains, 'Fall upon us!' and to the hills, 'Cover us!' for if these things are done when the wood is green what will happen when it is dry?" Now two others, both criminals, were led away with him to be executed.

When they came to the place called the Skull, they crucified him and the criminals there, one on his right, the other on his left. Then Jesus said, "Father, forgive them, they know not what they do." They divided his garments by casting lots. The people stood by and watched; the rulers, meanwhile, sneered at him and said, "He saved others, let him save himself if he is the chosen one, the Christ of God." Even the soldiers jeered at him. As they approached to offer him wine they called out, "If you are King of the Jews, save yourself." Above him there was an inscription that read, "This is the King of the Jews."

Now one of the criminals hanging there reviled Jesus, saying, "Are you not the Christ? Save yourself and us." The other, however, rebuking him, said in reply, "Have you no fear of God, for you are subject to the same condemnation? And indeed, we have been condemned justly, for the sentence we received corresponds to our crimes, but this man has done nothing criminal." Then he said, "Jesus, remember me when you come into your kingdom." He replied to him, "Amen, I say to you, today you will be with me in Paradise."

It was now about noon and darkness came over the whole land until three in the afternoon because of an eclipse of the sun. Then the veil of the temple was torn down the middle. Jesus cried out in a loud voice, "Father, into your hands I commend my spirit"; and when he had said this he breathed his last.

Here all kneel and pause for a short time.

The centurion who witnessed what had happened glorified God and said, "This man was innocent beyond doubt." When all the people who had gathered for this spectacle saw what had happened, they returned home beating their breasts; but all his acquaintances stood at a distance, including the women who had followed him from Galilee and saw these events.

Brief Silence

For Reflection

Luke emphasizes Jesus's role as prophet. He interprets Jesus's death as a rejection of his prophetic teaching and actions. Like all prophets, Jesus is lauded by those lifted up by his good news, but those whose privileged position is threatened by him seek to silence and kill him. In the passion narrative, we see Jesus facing deadly opposition and struggling one final time to discern the way to obediently bring his prophetic mission to completion. He prepares his disciples for his own death, instructing them at the Last Supper, and modeling for them how they are to act, as they continue his prophetic mission.

As followers of such a prophet, our own obedience is modeled on his. First, prophetic obedience is enacted by turning one's ear to God morning after morning. It also entails remembering, as Jesus said at the Last Supper—making present again his bold words and freeing actions of healing and forgiveness. As servant leaders, it also means going, like the Galilean women, to the places of death, keeping watch in solidarity with the crucified peoples of our world and continuing to protest the machinery of death, even as we ourselves risk falling victim to them.

✦ How can you stay mindful of God's presence even in the midst of suffering? How do you remember God through seasons of sorrow or pain?

Brief Silence

Prayer

The psalmist writes, "You open wide your hand and satisfy the desire of every living thing" (Ps 145:16). Loving God, give us grateful hearts to receive the gifts you share, trusting you provide us with all we need. In a special way, open our hearts to the gift of yourself in this Eucharist so that we might know you more fully, love you more deeply, and serve you more faithfully in all we do. **Amen.**

HOLY THURSDAY EVENING MASS OF THE LORD'S SUPPER

On this night, when Jesus cleansed his disciples' feet, we look to him for cleansing as we admit our faults and seek his forgiveness and consolation . . .

Prayer

Servant Lord, in the institution of the Eucharist, you gave us your body and blood, that we might remember your sacrifice for us. As we enter these holiest of days, may we strive always to imitate you, following your example of love and service to all. In your holy name we pray. **Amen**.

Gospel **John 13:1-15**

Before the feast of Passover, Jesus knew that his hour had come to pass from this world to the Father. He loved his own in the world and he loved them to the end. The devil had already induced Judas, son of Simon the Iscariot, to hand him over. So, during supper, fully aware that the Father had put everything into his power and that he had come from God and was returning to God, he rose from supper and took off his outer garments. He took a towel and tied it around his waist. Then he poured water into a basin and began to wash the disciples' feet and dry them with the towel around his waist. He came to Simon Peter, who said to him, "Master, are you going to wash my feet?" Jesus answered and said to him, "What I am doing, you do not understand now, but you will understand later." Peter said to him, "You will never wash my feet." Jesus answered him, "Unless I wash you, you will have no inheritance with me." Simon Peter said to him, "Master, then not only my feet, but my hands and head as well." Jesus said to him, "Whoever has bathed has no need except to have his feet washed, for he is clean all over; so you are clean, but not all." For he knew who would betray him; for this reason, he said, "Not all of you are clean."

So when he had washed their feet and put his garments back on and reclined at table again, he said to them, "Do you realize what I have done for you? You call me 'teacher' and 'master,' and rightly so, for indeed I am. If I, therefore, the master and teacher, have washed your feet, you ought to wash one another's feet. I have given you a model to follow, so that as I have done for you, you should also do."

Brief Silence

For Reflection

In today's gospel, Jesus hands on something central to the Christian life: loving service. Jesus knows that his time is at an end, that he is returning to the Father. So how does he respond? By stripping off his garments and bending down to wash feet. The God of all creation spends his final moments in human community serving those whom he loves. Are we willing to let God love us like this?

Jesus washes the apostles' feet as a sign and an instruction for them: "as I have done for you, you should also do." For us today, this signifying action of Jesus is a reminder that the eucharistic celebration is incomplete without a lived response. We ourselves must be incorporated into the very Body of Christ. Jesus asks in the gospel reading, "Do you realize what I have done for you?" What a powerful question. When we celebrate the Eucharist today for the last time before Easter, when we behold Christ's own body and blood, do we recognize what he has done for us? Do we live our lives in memory of his, handing on that which we have received?

✦ What is a task you find unpleasant? Could you see it as an act of love—even an act of participating in Christ's love? Does that change it for you?

Brief Silence

Prayer

The psalmist writes, "You open wide your hand and satisfy the desire of every living thing" (Ps 145:16). Loving God, give us grateful hearts to receive the gifts you share, trusting you provide us with all we need. In a special way, open our hearts to the gift of yourself in this Eucharist so that we might know you more fully, love you more deeply, and serve you more faithfully in all we do. **Amen.**

EASTER SUNDAY OF THE RESURRECTION (at the Mass during the Day)

Rejoicing in the glorious light of Easter day, we prepare to celebrate these sacred mysteries as we bring our hearts before the risen Lord . . .

Prayer

God of resurrection and new life, today we celebrate your triumph over the grave, and over death itself. Help us to live as Easter people, with a song of praise ever on our lips. This, indeed, is the day the Lord has made! In joy and with thanksgiving, we pray. **Amen**.

Gospel **John 20:1-9 (or Luke 24:1-12; or at an afternoon or evening Mass, Luke 24:13-35)**

On the first day of the week, Mary of Magdala came to the tomb early in the morning, while it was still dark, and saw the stone removed from the tomb. So she ran and went to Simon Peter and to the other disciple whom Jesus loved, and told them, "They have taken the Lord from the tomb, and we don't know where they put him." So Peter and the other disciple went out and came to the tomb. They both ran, but the other disciple ran faster than Peter and arrived at the tomb first; he bent down and saw the burial cloths there, but did not go in. When Simon Peter arrived after him, he went into the tomb and saw the burial cloths there, and the cloth that had covered his head, not with the burial cloths but rolled up in a separate place. Then the other disciple also went in, the one who had arrived at the tomb first, and he saw and believed. For they did not yet understand the Scripture that he had to rise from the dead.

Brief Silence

For Reflection

Everything depends on Easter morning. Is the tomb empty or is it not? Emerging from the dourness of Lent and the desolation of Good Friday, can we begin to recognize God present in our midst? Can we accept the invitation of Jesus to live in the joy of the resurrection?

Like Mary Magdalene, like Peter and the beloved disciple, when we encounter the risen Jesus, we are called to proclaim the gospel, the good news. The resurrection of Christ at Easter is a message that must be broadcast through all space and time. Easter is the final triumph of life over death, of love over evil, of God's kingdom over tyranny and oppression. That is good news the world needs to hear. Do we live as if Christ has truly risen from the dead? Are we willing to share this good news with others, like Peter does in our first reading? Like Paul does in his letters? God has already won our salvation, our freedom in Christ Jesus our Lord. What else is there for us to do than to share this gospel with all we encounter?

✦ What hints of Jesus's resurrection do you see in your own life? Where have you witnessed life and healing, and how do they speak to you of God's presence?

Brief Silence

Prayer

The psalmist writes, "You open wide your hand and satisfy the desire of every living thing" (Ps 145:16). Loving God, give us grateful hearts to receive the gifts you share, trusting you provide us with all we need. In a special way, open our hearts to the gift of yourself in this Eucharist so that we might know you more fully, love you more deeply, and serve you more faithfully in all we do. **Amen.**

SECOND SUNDAY OF EASTER (OR DIVINE MERCY SUNDAY)

Today's reading from Acts assures us of God's cure for our ailments; let us now approach God in repentance for those times when sin has brought the need for healing . . .

Prayer

Lord Jesus, in your first resurrected encounter with your disciples you said to them, "Peace be with you." May we embrace your promise of peace and choose to believe in you, especially during the times when we cannot see your hand at work in our lives. Jesus, we trust in you, and in your holy name we pray. **Amen.**

Gospel **John 20:19-31**

On the evening of that first day of the week, when the doors were locked, where the disciples were, for fear of the Jews, Jesus came and stood in their midst and said to them, "Peace be with you." When he had said this, he showed them his hands and his side. The disciples rejoiced when they saw the Lord. Jesus said to them again, "Peace be with you. As the Father has sent me, so I send you." And when he had said this, he breathed on them and said to them, "Receive the Holy Spirit. Whose sins you forgive are forgiven them, and whose sins you retain are retained."

Thomas, called Didymus, one of the Twelve, was not with them when Jesus came. So the other disciples said to him, "We have seen the Lord." But he said to them, "Unless I see the mark of the nails in his hands and put my finger into the nailmarks and put my hand into his side, I will not believe."

Now a week later his disciples were again inside and Thomas was with them. Jesus came, although the doors were locked, and stood in their midst and said, "Peace be with you." Then he said to Thomas, "Put your finger here and see my hands, and bring your hand and put it into my side, and do not be unbelieving, but believe." Thomas answered and said to him, "My Lord and my God!" Jesus said to him, "Have you come to believe because you have seen me? Blessed are those who have not seen and have believed."

Now, Jesus did many other signs in the presence of his disciples that are not written in this book. But these are written that you may come to believe that Jesus is the Christ, the Son of God, and that through this belief you may have life in his name.

Brief Silence

For Reflection

In the Gospel of John, the risen Jesus equips the disciples with everything they need to continue his mission. First, he opens the locked doors of their hearts to recognize that he is standing in their midst. He had assured them that he would not leave them orphaned (14:18) and that he would abide always with them (15:4-10). He had also told them he would give them a peace unlike the peace that the world gives (14:27).

As the risen Christ stands in their midst, we see that his peace comes from letting go of fear and the desire for vengeance, and from surrounding the violence with forgiveness and reconciliation. This kind of peace does not ignore the brutal suffering inflicted on the victim. Jesus holds out his wounded hands and side as evidence that it is never erased. The pain from the violence can be transformed, however, into joy and peace, through the power of the Spirit and through the abiding presence of God, who makes possible forgiveness.

Not all follow the same process toward embracing the peace Christ extends. As the scene with Thomas affirms, disciples encounter the risen Christ at different times and in different ways.

✦ Is there anything holding you back from participating fully in the church's joy this Easter season? How could your community support you in your grief or pain?

SECOND SUNDAY OF EASTER (OR DIVINE MERCY SUNDAY)

Brief Silence

Prayer

The psalmist writes, "You open wide your hand and satisfy the desire of every living thing" (Ps 145:16). Loving God, give us grateful hearts to receive the gifts you share, trusting you provide us with all we need. In a special way, open our hearts to the gift of yourself in this Eucharist so that we might know you more fully, love you more deeply, and serve you more faithfully in all we do. **Amen.**

The Lord appears to the disciples again, making himself known in the breaking of the bread and calling them to follow him. Following our desire to know and come to Christ, we ask for his loving mercy . . .

Prayer

Lord Jesus, you know everything: you know that we love you. Give us the strength to preach your gospel, even as the apostles did when ordered not to. May we always show our desire to follow you by being faithful to your word and feeding your sheep. In your name we pray. **Amen.**

Gospel **John 21:1-19 (or John 21:1-14)**

At that time, Jesus revealed himself again to his disciples at the Sea of Tiberias. He revealed himself in this way. Together were Simon Peter, Thomas called Didymus, Nathanael from Cana in Galilee, Zebedee's sons, and two others of his disciples. Simon Peter said to them, "I am going fishing." They said to him, "We also will come with you." So they went out and got into the boat, but that night they caught nothing. When it was already dawn, Jesus was standing on the shore; but the disciples did not realize that it was Jesus. Jesus said to them, "Children, have you caught anything to eat?" They answered him, "No." So he said to them, "Cast the net over the right side of the boat and you will find something." So they cast it, and were not able to pull it in because of the number of fish. So the disciple whom Jesus loved said to Peter, "It is the Lord." When Simon Peter heard that it was the Lord, he tucked in his garment, for he was lightly clad, and jumped into the sea. The other disciples came in the boat, for they were not far from shore, only about a hundred yards, dragging the net with the fish. When they climbed out on shore, they saw a charcoal fire with fish on it and bread. Jesus said to them, "Bring some of the fish you just caught." So Simon Peter went over and dragged the net ashore full of one hundred fifty-three large fish. Even though there were so many, the net was not torn. Jesus said to them, "Come, have breakfast." And none of the disciples dared to ask him, "Who are you?" because they realized it was the Lord. Jesus came over and took the bread and gave it to them, and in like manner the fish. This was now the third time Jesus was revealed to his disciples after being raised from the dead.

When they had finished breakfast, Jesus said to Simon Peter, "Simon, son of John, do you love me more than these?" Simon Peter answered him, "Yes, Lord, you know that I love you." Jesus said to him, "Feed my lambs." He then said to Simon Peter a second time, "Simon, son of John, do you love me?" Simon Peter answered him, "Yes, Lord, you know that I love you." Jesus said to him, "Tend my sheep." Jesus said to him the third time, "Simon, son of John, do you love me?" Peter was distressed that Jesus had said to him a third time, "Do you love me?" and he said to him, "Lord, you know everything; you know that I love you." Jesus said to him, "Feed my sheep. Amen, amen, I say to you, when you were younger, you used to dress yourself and go where you wanted; but when you grow old, you will stretch out your hands, and someone else will dress you and lead you where you do not want to go." He said this signifying by what kind of death he would glorify God. And when he had said this, he said to him, "Follow me."

Brief Silence

For Reflection

At a parish liturgy, a couple married for fifty years renews their marital promises. In a Mass held the same day at a nearby convent, a group of sisters publicly renews their vows. The commitment to love is not something professed only once, but again and again. Recalling one's first fervor of infatuation with the Beloved fans into flame again the ability to continue loving despite hardships and challenges.

So it is with Peter in today's gospel. When pressed by a servant girl, he had failed to acknowledge that he even knew Jesus. Earlier, at the tumultuous moment of Jesus's arrest, he had hotheadedly lashed out with a sword and had cut off the ear of a slave of the high priest. His failures to love are symbolically depicted in his inability to catch any fish.

Yet Peter still does love Jesus and is still able to bring many others into that circle of love. Allowing himself to be fed by the Source of love, he experiences forgiveness, renewal, and empowerment to extend that love to others. It is an efficacious and uniting love, symbolized by the great haul of fish and the net that is not torn.

✦ Like Peter, our journeys with Christ are bound to have ups and downs. Where do you feel you are in your faith journey? What would help you to grow into a mature faith willing to endure suffering for Christ?

Brief Silence

Prayer

The psalmist writes, "You open wide your hand and satisfy the desire of every living thing" (Ps 145:16). Loving God, give us grateful hearts to receive the gifts you share, trusting you provide us with all we need. In a special way, open our hearts to the gift of yourself in this Eucharist so that we might know you more fully, love you more deeply, and serve you more faithfully in all we do. **Amen.**

Today, we are reminded that we are to make Christ known to the ends of the earth, serving as a light to the nations. Calling to mind the times we have failed to be as Christ would have us be, we ask for his pardon and peace . . .

Prayer

Lord Jesus, you are the good shepherd. You made us, and in faith we profess that we belong to you. Thank you for calling us each by name and giving us life. Despite our failings and our unworthiness, we are grateful to be called your children, and we strive to follow you always. Trusting in you, we pray. **Amen**.

Gospel **John 10:27-30**

Jesus said: "My sheep hear my voice; I know them, and they follow me. I give them eternal life, and they shall never perish. No one can take them out of my hand. My Father, who has given them to me, is greater than all, and no one can take them out of the Father's hand. The Father and I are one."

Brief Silence

For Reflection

The Lamb in the Gospel of John is the Passover lamb, whose bones are not broken (Exod 12:46; John 19:36), whose blood, as in the exodus, protects his people from the destroyer, and whose flesh fortifies his own for their journey to freedom. This is the one whose blood came forth from his pierced side, along with waters of rebirth (19:34), cleansing, renewing, and opening the way to new life for all. Paradoxically, the Lamb is also—as we see in today's gospel reading—the shepherd, whose sheep respond to the sound of his voice, and from whose hands no one can snatch his sheep.

In the book of Revelation, the Lamb is now enthroned in glory, clothing everyone in the resplendent robe of his life and love. The blood that washes over each is the life force unleashed by the crucified Jesus and infused into his followers by the Spirit. It does not whitewash the shedding of blood from racism and other forms of sin but empowers all who are bloodied in the earthly struggles to emerge cleansed in his loving life force.

✦ How do you hear the voice of Jesus? Which parts of following Jesus are easy for you? Which present a challenge at this point in your life?

Brief Silence

Prayer

The psalmist writes, "You open wide your hand and satisfy the desire of every living thing" (Ps 145:16). Loving God, give us grateful hearts to receive the gifts you share, trusting you provide us with all we need. In a special way, open our hearts to the gift of yourself in this Eucharist so that we might know you more fully, love you more deeply, and serve you more faithfully in all we do. **Amen.**

FIFTH SUNDAY OF EASTER

The Lord gives us a new commandment to love one another as he has loved us. Being mindful of the times we have failed to love as we should, we ask for his pardon and peace . . .

Prayer

Lord Jesus, in your death and resurrection, you have made all things new, and for this we praise your name. You even gave us a new commandment: may we show the world that we are truly your disciples by loving others as you have taught us to do. For the strength and the courage to love, we pray. **Amen**.

Gospel **John 13:31-33a, 34-35**

When Judas had left them, Jesus said, "Now is the Son of Man glorified, and God is glorified in him. If God is glorified in him, God will also glorify him in himself, and God will glorify him at once. My children, I will be with you only a little while longer. I give you a new commandment: love one another. As I have loved you, so you also should love one another. This is how all will know that you are my disciples, if you have love for one another."

Brief Silence

For Reflection

Jesus's command to love one another is part of his explanation to the disciples of his washing their feet. He has modeled for them actions that bespeak love—a love that will even go so far as to surrender life itself for the other. It is a love that is extended even to those who will not reciprocate it.

Jesus not only gives the disciples the gift of his love; he also commands them to do as he has done. He has shown what love is by acting it out—pouring out himself in service, even to calamity's depths. When we see Jesus's love in action, it becomes evident how love can be commanded.

In biblical parlance, love does not consist in warm, fuzzy feelings toward another but in visible acts that bespeak a shared divine parentage and common commitment to one another. To love as Jesus loves, it's not necessary to like or even feel kindly toward the other person. But it is necessary to act toward the other in the way Jesus treated his disciples as he washed their feet. Sometimes loving feelings result from loving action extended and received.

✦ In this gospel, Jesus begins to prepare his disciples for his departure. What do you need to hear from Jesus to prepare for times in life when he will be hard to see?

Brief Silence

Prayer

The psalmist writes, "You open wide your hand and satisfy the desire of every living thing" (Ps 145:16). Loving God, give us grateful hearts to receive the gifts you share, trusting you provide us with all we need. In a special way, open our hearts to the gift of yourself in this Eucharist so that we might know you more fully, love you more deeply, and serve you more faithfully in all we do. **Amen.**

In the gospel today, Jesus encourages us not to let our hearts be troubled or afraid. Let us begin by turning our hearts to him, preparing for his mercy and peace . . .

Prayer

Lord Jesus, in your last days with the disciples, you told them not to be troubled or afraid and again said, "Peace." We trust in your promise of the Advocate to guide us, and we rejoice in your dwelling with us. Let all the peoples praise you, O Lord! In your holy name we pray. **Amen**.

Gospel **John 14:23-29**

Jesus said to his disciples: "Whoever loves me will keep my word, and my Father will love him, and we will come to him and make our dwelling with him. Whoever does not love me does not keep my words; yet the word you hear is not mine but that of the Father who sent me.

"I have told you this while I am with you. The Advocate, the Holy Spirit, whom the Father will send in my name, will teach you everything and remind you of all that I told you. Peace I leave with you; my peace I give to you. Not as the world gives do I give it to you. Do not let your hearts be troubled or afraid. You heard me tell you, 'I am going away and I will come back to you.' If you loved me, you would rejoice that I am going to the Father; for the Father is greater than I. And now I have told you this before it happens, so that when it happens you may believe."

Brief Silence

For Reflection

Frequently, the only time the Holy Spirit features in our parishes is at Pentecost and when we celebrate the sacrament of confirmation. The Third Person of the Trinity deserves so much more attention than that!

At the Last Supper, Jesus promises that "we [my Father and I] will come to him [whoever loves me] and make our dwelling with him." Even as Jesus speaks of his departure, he promises the presence of God—not in a physical presence, but in a greater way. Jesus promises that his own Spirit will come to make his dwelling with us. Indeed, this is the Spirit that "proceeds from the Father and the Son." The love between the Father and the Son overflows such that it becomes its own coequal Person, the very Spirit that resides within each of us by our baptism. It is in the Spirit that we come to be children of God the Father, with Christ Jesus as our brother. This is the nearness to each of us that Jesus promises in this gospel passage—a bond greater than any other.

✦ What makes it hard for you to trust in the peace Jesus promises? What in this life leaves you troubled or afraid?

Brief Silence

Prayer

The psalmist writes, "You open wide your hand and satisfy the desire of every living thing" (Ps 145:16). Loving God, give us grateful hearts to receive the gifts you share, trusting you provide us with all we need. In a special way, open our hearts to the gift of yourself in this Eucharist so that we might know you more fully, love you more deeply, and serve you more faithfully in all we do. **Amen.**

Today's readings remind us that the Holy Spirit calls us to repentance and a new way of life. Aware of our need to turn away from sin, we call upon the mercy of our God . . .

Prayer

Lord Jesus, like your disciples, we praise you and do you homage as you ascend to your holy place. Grant us the courage to be your witnesses throughout the world, that your sacrifice and your enduring love for us might be known to all peoples. We ask this in your holy name. **Amen.**

Gospel **Luke 24:46-53**

Jesus said to his disciples: "Thus it is written that the Christ would suffer and rise from the dead on the third day and that repentance, for the forgiveness of sins, would be preached in his name to all the nations, beginning from Jerusalem. You are witnesses of these things. And behold I am sending the promise of my Father upon you; but stay in the city until you are clothed with power from on high."

Then he led them out as far as Bethany, raised his hands, and blessed them. As he blessed them he parted from them and was taken up to heaven. They did him homage and then returned to Jerusalem with great joy, and they were continually in the temple praising God.

Brief Silence

For Reflection

In her book *Wouldn't Take Nothing for My Journey Now*, poet Maya Angelou recalls the grandmother who raised her. Angelou writes that Mamma would look up into a distant sky and declare, "I will step out on the word of God." She continues, "She would look up as if she could will herself into the heavens. . . . I could see her flung into space, moons at her feet and stars at her head, comets swirling around her."

In today's readings, we have similar images of Jesus "taken up" into the sky, having spent an earthly lifetime stepping out on the word of God. The disciples want to know if now is the time that he is going to restore the kingdom to Israel (Acts 1:6). They have hopes and expectations for the future fixed in past experiences of God's saving hand in their history. Jesus points them to the power of the Holy Spirit, with which they will be clothed. This power will guide them so that they'll be able to step out on the word that has been entrusted to them, courageously witnessing to the gospel from Jerusalem to the ends of the earth.

✦ What does it mean to you to be a witness? How do you bear witness to the work God has done in your own life?

Brief Silence

Prayer

The psalmist writes, "You open wide your hand and satisfy the desire of every living thing" (Ps 145:16). Loving God, give us grateful hearts to receive the gifts you share, trusting you provide us with all we need. In a special way, open our hearts to the gift of yourself in this Eucharist so that we might know you more fully, love you more deeply, and serve you more faithfully in all we do. **Amen.**

John's gospel tells us that we are called to be one with Christ and the Father. For those times that we have separated ourselves from our God, let us ask for his pardon and peace . . .

Prayer

Lord Jesus, you and the Father are one, and you have loved us as the Father loves you. As you now reign in heaven, may we strive ever more fully to live as one, to be brought to perfection in you, and to make you known on earth. Glorifying your name, we pray. **Amen.**

Gospel **John 17:20-26**

Lifting up his eyes to heaven, Jesus prayed, saying: "Holy Father, I pray not only for them, but also for those who will believe in me through their word, so that they may all be one, as you, Father, are in me and I in you, that they also may be in us, that the world may believe that you sent me. And I have given them the glory you gave me, so that they may be one, as we are one, I in them and you in me, that they may be brought to perfection as one, that the world may know that you sent me, and that you loved them even as you loved me. Father, they are your gift to me. I wish that where I am they also may be with me, that they may see my glory that you gave me, because you loved me before the foundation of the world. Righteous Father, the world also does not know you, but I know you, and they know that you sent me. I made known to them your name and I will make it known, that the love with which you loved me may be in them and I in them."

Brief Silence

For Reflection

In today's gospel passage Jesus speaks of his profound oneness with the Father that he desires to share completely with those who believe in him. As we are becoming more aware in our day of the oneness of the whole cosmos, we may hear Jesus's prayer not only for oneness of the human community but also for every part of the created universe. We know that every part of the cosmos is interrelated and connected in one great web of life and that we are physically connected by atoms that have recycled into us from other living beings.

Since this is our reality, perhaps Jesus's prayer is not so much a prayer that unity may come to be, but rather that we who are already completely and irrevocably united may come to this realization and act accordingly. This realization would have a profound effect not only on how human beings treat one another but also on the ways in which human beings care for Earth and all creatures.

✦ In the gospel, Jesus calls his followers God's gift to him. Do you think of yourself as a gift to Jesus? How might you make your life into a gift to him?

Brief Silence

Prayer

The psalmist writes, "You open wide your hand and satisfy the desire of every living thing" (Ps 145:16). Loving God, give us grateful hearts to receive the gifts you share, trusting you provide us with all we need. In a special way, open our hearts to the gift of yourself in this Eucharist so that we might know you more fully, love you more deeply, and serve you more faithfully in all we do. **Amen.**

We have a God who sent the Spirit of truth to guide his people. Confident that he is always with us in love and mercy, we turn to him mindful of those times when we have strayed from his ways . . .

Prayer

God of all giving, you sent the Son to us to show us the way to you, and you sent the Spirit to remind us of all Jesus taught us. Led by that same Spirit, may we always remember that we are your children, brothers and sisters in Christ Jesus. And together we pray, "Come, Holy Spirit!" **Amen**.

Gospel **John 20:19-23; or John 14:15-16, 23b-26; At the Mass during the Day**

On the evening of that first day of the week, when the doors were locked, where the disciples were, for fear of the Jews, Jesus came and stood in their midst and said to them, "Peace be with you." When he had said this, he showed them his hands and his side. The disciples rejoiced when they saw the Lord. Jesus said to them again, "Peace be with you. As the Father has sent me, so I send you." And when he had said this, he breathed on them and said to them, "Receive the Holy Spirit. Whose sins you forgive are forgiven them, and whose sins you retain are retained."

Brief Silence

For Reflection

In John 20 (one of the two possible choices for today's gospel reading), the risen Christ breathes on the disciples and infuses them with the Spirit. He unleashes in them the power of the Spirit, who alone can bring peace and joy in the wake of terrifying woundedness. He directs them to open themselves to the gift of the Spirit that allows them to receive and give forgiveness. For it is only through the power of forgiveness that the air can be cleared and all can breathe in the peace for which we so long and which the risen One desires to give.

Perhaps it is breath that best signals this intimacy. God, in the person of Jesus and the power of the Spirit, is as close to each and every believer as is our very breath, taken deeply into our lungs thousands of times every day, a constant vivifying force. Just as breath must be exhaled, and cannot be kept within, so too does the Spirit's power direct us outward to mission, exuding the love, peace, and forgiveness we have inhaled from the Living One.

✦ Our theological tradition names seven gifts of the Holy Spirit: wisdom, understanding, counsel, fortitude, knowledge, piety, and fear of the Lord. Which of these do you most need right now?

Brief Silence

Prayer

The psalmist writes, "You open wide your hand and satisfy the desire of every living thing" (Ps 145:16). Loving God, give us grateful hearts to receive the gifts you share, trusting you provide us with all we need. In a special way, open our hearts to the gift of yourself in this Eucharist so that we might know you more fully, love you more deeply, and serve you more faithfully in all we do. **Amen.**

Today, Scripture assures us that God brings us to the truth. For those times that we have veered from what is true and good, let us seek God's pardon and peace . . .

Prayer

Creator God, we give thanks that we are wonderfully made. Redeemer God, we give thanks for your passion and death, which have brought us to new life. Sanctifying God, we give thanks for your enduring presence. And we thank you, Three-in-One, for the example of love that you show us. In the name of our triune God, we pray. **Amen.**

Gospel **John 16:12-15**

Jesus said to his disciples: "I have much more to tell you, but you cannot bear it now. But when he comes, the Spirit of truth, he will guide you to all truth. He will not speak on his own, but he will speak what he hears, and will declare to you the things that are coming. He will glorify me, because he will take from what is mine and declare it to you. Everything that the Father has is mine; for this reason I told you that he will take from what is mine and declare it to you."

Brief Silence

For Reflection

Mi casa es su casa—"My home is your home"—is the greeting extended to visitors in many Hispanic households. The hospitality offered is boundless, as hosts outdo themselves in generosity, eager to share with guests everything they have.

In some ways this example of persons who pour out themselves in generosity to others gives us a glimpse of the relationship among the persons of the Trinity and of their outpouring of love for us. In today's gospel reading Jesus has been speaking with his disciples about the Paraclete that will come when he departs. As he describes all that the Paraclete, the Spirit, will be and do, we recognize these as the very things that comprised Jesus's person and mission. Jesus explains that the Spirit "will take from what is mine and declare it to you." But what is Jesus's is also what is the Father's, as Jesus asserts, "Everything that the Father has is mine." There is no "yours and mine" in the Godhead—only "ours," as the three interweave in a communion of love in which there is no possessiveness.

✦ The Trinity's love pours out as life-giving creativity. What are some wonders of the natural world that draw your attention to God?

Brief Silence

Prayer

The psalmist writes, "You open wide your hand and satisfy the desire of every living thing" (Ps 145:16). Loving God, give us grateful hearts to receive the gifts you share, trusting you provide us with all we need. In a special way, open our hearts to the gift of yourself in this Eucharist so that we might know you more fully, love you more deeply, and serve you more faithfully in all we do. **Amen.**

THE MOST HOLY BODY AND BLOOD OF CHRIST (CORPUS CHRISTI)

We come before the Lord who has called us to his heavenly feast. Let us prepare ourselves to celebrate this Eucharist and the eternal banquet that awaits us by calling to mind our need for his mercy . . .

Prayer

God of abundance, through your miraculous power, you fed the five thousand with just a few loaves and fishes. Through the mystery of the Eucharist, we are fed with the very body and blood of Christ. May these gifts sustain us in our pilgrimage here on earth and lead us to everlasting life. Through Christ, our Lord. **Amen**.

Gospel **Luke 9:11b-17**

Jesus spoke to the crowds about the kingdom of God, and he healed those who needed to be cured. As the day was drawing to a close, the Twelve approached him and said, "Dismiss the crowd so that they can go to the surrounding villages and farms and find lodging and provisions; for we are in a deserted place here." He said to them, "Give them some food yourselves." They replied, "Five loaves and two fish are all we have, unless we ourselves go and buy food for all these people." Now the men there numbered about five thousand. Then he said to his disciples, "Have them sit down in groups of about fifty." They did so and made them all sit down. Then taking the five loaves and the two fish, and looking up to heaven, he said the blessing over them, broke them, and gave them to the disciples to set before the crowd. They all ate and were satisfied. And when the leftover fragments were picked up, they filled twelve wicker baskets.

Brief Silence

For Reflection

Today's feast day celebrates the gift of Christ, who entrusted his entire self to us, in his life and ministry but especially in his self-surrender in death.

In the gospel, we see how easy it is to miss the moment when such self-gift is asked of us. The crowds have been with Jesus all day. Now they are tired and hungry, and the Twelve suggest to Jesus that he send the crowd into the surrounding villages to get food.

Instead, Jesus directs the Twelve to their own resources. He takes the five loaves and two fish, looks up to heaven, blesses, breaks, and gives them to the disciples to set before the crowd. There is plenty for all and then some. The miracle is a summons to the giving of our whole selves to the One who is the Source of all nourishment so that we may be broken open in love for the life of the world.

Such self-giving is not possible on our own. It is in the gathered assembly of believers, where we remember Christ's act in sacramental ritual, that we gain strength and give courage to one another to entrust ourselves to this kind of love.

✦ What has the Eucharist meant to you at different points on your journey of faith?

Brief Silence

Prayer

The psalmist writes, "You open wide your hand and satisfy the desire of every living thing" (Ps 145:16). Loving God, give us grateful hearts to receive the gifts you share, trusting you provide us with all we need. In a special way, open our hearts to the gift of yourself in this Eucharist so that we might know you more fully, love you more deeply, and serve you more faithfully in all we do. **Amen.**

THE NATIVITY OF SAINT JOHN THE BAPTIST

John heralded the coming of Jesus by proclaiming a baptism of repentance. Remembering the grace we first received at our baptism, let us call to mind our sins and ask for God's pardon and peace . . .

Prayer

Miraculous God, may we allow the example of John the Baptist to convince us to keep our eyes and ears open to the prompting of the Holy Spirit. **Amen**.

Gospel **Luke 1:57-66, 80**

When the time arrived for Elizabeth to have her child she gave birth to a son. Her neighbors and relatives heard that the Lord had shown his great mercy toward her, and they rejoiced with her. When they came on the eighth day to circumcise the child, they were going to call him Zechariah after his father, but his mother said in reply, "No. He will be called John." But they answered her, "There is no one among your relatives who has this name." So they made signs, asking his father what he wished him to be called. He asked for a tablet and wrote, "John is his name," and all were amazed. Immediately his mouth was opened, his tongue freed, and he spoke blessing God. Then fear came upon all their neighbors, and all these matters were discussed throughout the hill country of Judea. All who heard these things took them to heart, saying, "What, then, will this child be?" For surely the hand of the Lord was with him.

The child grew and became strong in spirit, and he was in the desert until the day of his manifestation to Israel.

Brief Silence

For Reflection

John the Baptist's entire life and ministry are a sign pointing toward the saving mission of Jesus our Lord. John the Forerunner is the last of the prophets of Israel, who in their time spoke of God's future deliverance. John's baptism in the Jordan is a precursor to a greater baptism to come. Even John's death at the hands of Herod to appease the people foreshadows the death of Jesus at the hands of Pilate to satisfy the Passover crowds. In all things John pointed to Christ in humility: "He must increase; I must decrease" (John 3:30). We have much to learn from the example of John. How can we live our lives as signs pointing to the love of Christ? Are we willing to decrease, so that Christ can increase in us?

God is not passive but is constantly at motion in the world. Do we strive to see God in our lives? Do we respond to the voice of God in our hearts? Or are we like Zechariah, refusing to recognize the goodness of God at work? If we recognize God's love among us, may we respond as Zechariah at last does, with a hymn of praise, and may we, like John the Baptist, "prepare the way of the Lord."

✦ John the Baptist comes before Christ, preparing his listeners to receive the fulfillment of God's promises. Who in your life has helped point you to Christ? Who has prepared you to encounter God?

Brief Silence

Prayer

The psalmist writes, "You open wide your hand and satisfy the desire of every living thing" (Ps 145:16). Loving God, give us grateful hearts to receive the gifts you share, trusting you provide us with all we need. In a special way, open our hearts to the gift of yourself in this Eucharist so that we might know you more fully, love you more deeply, and serve you more faithfully in all we do. **Amen.**

SAINTS PETER AND PAUL, APOSTLES

Today we celebrate Saints Peter and Paul, both of whom experienced forgiveness and transformation in Christ. May we follow their example as we come before the Lord asking for his mercy . . .

Prayer

Almighty God, Saint Paul encountered you on the road to Damascus, and his life was radically changed; may we also encounter you and find ourselves transformed. You released Saint Peter from his chains; free us from the ties that bind us, that we might build your kingdom here on earth. We ask these things through Christ, our Lord. **Amen.**

Gospel **Matt 16:13-19**

When Jesus went into the region of Caesarea Philippi he asked his disciples, "Who do people say that the Son of Man is?" They replied, "Some say John the Baptist, others Elijah, still others Jeremiah or one of the prophets." He said to them, "But who do you say that I am?" Simon Peter said in reply, "You are the Christ, the Son of the living God." Jesus said to him in reply, "Blessed are you, Simon son of Jonah. For flesh and blood has not revealed this to you, but my heavenly Father. And so I say to you, you are Peter, and upon this rock I will build my Church, and the gates of the netherworld shall not prevail against it. I will give you the keys to the Kingdom of heaven. Whatever you bind on earth shall be bound in heaven; and whatever you loose on earth shall be loosed in heaven."

Brief Silence

For Reflection

In today's gospel, Jesus asks, "Who do you say that I am?" How would we answer this question? Maybe we'd respond like the "some" referenced by the apostles—Jesus is a nice person a good moral teacher, someone who tells us to all get along. Alternatively, maybe we'd repeat something formulaic from the Catechism or a theology textbook—Jesus is the Second Person of the Trinity, two natures in one person, and so on. Peter finds that Jesus is not satisfied with such an answer from others. Jesus probes further—who am I *to you?* Peter knows his response: "You are the Christ, the Son of the living God." A bold claim, and one that will have consequences for the rest of his life.

Today is a solemnity because of the significance of both Peter and Paul, two of the most important figures in the early church. Who could have guessed that a Galilean fisherman and a Pharisee from Tarsus could change the course of world history? Together, these great saints root the church firmly in the city of Rome—both ministered and were killed there. They also demonstrate that God qualifies the called rather than the other way around.

✦ What suffering have you had to endure for the sake of your faith? How has Jesus helped you get through it?

Brief Silence

Prayer

The psalmist writes, "You open wide your hand and satisfy the desire of every living thing" (Ps 145:16). Loving God, give us grateful hearts to receive the gifts you share, trusting you provide us with all we need. In a special way, open our hearts to the gift of yourself in this Eucharist so that we might know you more fully, love you more deeply, and serve you more faithfully in all we do. **Amen.**

FOURTEENTH SUNDAY IN ORDINARY TIME

We are called to allow the peace of Christ to control our hearts. For the times we have failed to listen to his word, we ask for his mercy . . .

Prayer

O God, all the earth cries out to you with joy! In you, we find comfort; through you, we experience peace. As Jesus appointed the seventy-two to preach his message, we ask you also to send us, so that we can share your grace, love, and mercy with others. Through Christ, our Lord. **Amen**.

Gospel **Luke 10:1-12, 17-20 (or Luke 10:1-9)**

At that time the Lord appointed seventy-two others whom he sent ahead of him in pairs to every town and place he intended to visit. He said to them, "The harvest is abundant but the laborers are few; so ask the master of the harvest to send out laborers for his harvest. Go on your way; behold, I am sending you like lambs among wolves. Carry no money bag, no sack, no sandals; and greet no one along the way. Into whatever house you enter, first say, 'Peace to this household.' If a peaceful person lives there, your peace will rest on him; but if not, it will return to you. Stay in the same house and eat and drink what is offered to you, for the laborer deserves his payment. Do not move about from one house to another. Whatever town you enter and they welcome you, eat what is set before you, cure the sick in it and say to them, 'The kingdom of God is at hand for you.' Whatever town you enter and they do not receive you, go out into the streets and say, 'The dust of your town that clings to our feet, even that we shake off against you.' Yet know this: the kingdom of God is at hand. I tell you, it will be more tolerable for Sodom on that day than for that town."

The seventy-two returned rejoicing, and said, "Lord, even the demons are subject to us because of your name." Jesus said, "I have observed Satan fall like lightning from the sky. Behold, I have given you the power to 'tread upon serpents' and scorpions and upon the full force of the enemy and nothing will harm you. Nevertheless, do not rejoice because the spirits are subject to you, but rejoice because your names are written in heaven."

Brief Silence

For Reflection

You may have read about the Mexican migrant farmworkers who do jobs that most Americans won't do. Harvesting lettuce, for example, they endure intense pains in their back and hands and arms; they skip water breaks despite the hot sun to keep up with bosses' expectations.

In today's gospel Jesus invites his disciples to take up the strenuous work of evangelization. As in the lettuce fields, the harvest is abundant, but those willing to take on this demanding work are few. Those who do are "like lambs among wolves," gentle and loving, while facing fierce opposition. Like migrant workers, whose presence is unwanted yet whose work is indispensable, laborers in God's vineyard also face frequent rejection.

The last part of the gospel points to the rewarding aspects of this difficult work. When proclaimers of the gospel see that their work can transform evil situations, the ensuing joy is indescribable. It is essential, however, that they not focus on the visible results of their handiwork nor take false pride in what they have accomplished. Their true joy comes from acknowledging the divine source of any success, as they entrust themselves fully to the One who has called them to mission.

✦ Jesus instructs his disciples to travel without even the basic comforts of travel; they are to rely instead on the hospitality of strangers. Where could you detach from some comfort in order to realize more fully your dependence on God?

Brief Silence

FOURTEENTH SUNDAY IN ORDINARY TIME

Prayer

The psalmist writes, "You open wide your hand and satisfy the desire of every living thing" (Ps 145:16). Loving God, give us grateful hearts to receive the gifts you share, trusting you provide us with all we need. In a special way, open our hearts to the gift of yourself in this Eucharist so that we might know you more fully, love you more deeply, and serve you more faithfully in all we do. **Amen.**

FIFTEENTH SUNDAY IN ORDINARY TIME

In our first reading today, Moses tells the people of Israel, "If only you would heed the voice of the LORD, your God, and keep his commandments and statutes." Turning to Christ who gives us a new commandment, we call to mind the times we have failed to heed his voice . . .

Prayer

Merciful God, you sent your Son to us so he could show us how to love. Even so, we need to be reminded to return to you again and again. May we more eagerly listen to your voice and heed your call, so that we might show others your great compassion. In Jesus's name we pray. **Amen**.

Gospel **Luke 10:25-37**

There was a scholar of the law who stood up to test Jesus and said, "Teacher, what must I do to inherit eternal life?" Jesus said to him, "What is written in the law? How do you read it?" He said in reply, *"You shall love the Lord, your God, with all your heart, with all your being, with all your strength, and with all your mind, and your neighbor as yourself."* He replied to him, "You have answered correctly; do this and you will live."

But because he wished to justify himself, he said to Jesus, "And who is my neighbor?" Jesus replied, "A man fell victim to robbers as he went down from Jerusalem to Jericho. They stripped and beat him and went off leaving him half-dead. A priest happened to be going down that road, but when he saw him, he passed by on the opposite side. Likewise a Levite came to the place, and when he saw him, he passed by on the opposite side. But a Samaritan traveler who came upon him was moved with compassion at the sight. He approached the victim, poured oil and wine over his wounds and bandaged them. Then he lifted him up on his own animal, took him to an inn, and cared for him. The next day he took out two silver coins and gave them to the innkeeper with the instruction, 'Take care of him. If you spend more than what I have given you, I shall repay you on my way back.' Which of these three, in your opinion, was neighbor to the robbers' victim?" He answered, "The one who treated him with mercy." Jesus said to him, "Go and do likewise."

Brief Silence

For Reflection

The question for the scholar of the law in today's gospel is not really "who is my neighbor?" Deep down he knows that each human being is neighbor and kin. The scholar doesn't want to admit this to himself because of what it will ask of him. In the depths of his heart, however, he knows what he must do to aid a fellow traveler in need. It is not really too hard or too mysterious to figure out, as Moses tells the Israelites in the first reading. How to live out God's way is actually "something very near to you, already in your mouths and in your hearts; you have only to carry it out," as Moses asserts.

Sometimes we need to be helped out of our rationalizations for not doing what our listening heart prompts us to do. At other times we are asked to be the one who can speak truth lovingly to a friend who struggles to do what compassion asks of him or her.

Heeding the voice of God to know the right action requires listening in prayer and in honest conversation with trusted friends and openness to hearing the cacophonous cries of needy neighbors.

✦ The scholar who questions Jesus is trying to ascertain the bare minimum he can do and still enter eternal life; Jesus calls him rather to a radical change of heart. Where do you struggle to give your whole heart to Jesus? How might he be inviting you to more fully follow him?

Brief Silence

FIFTEENTH SUNDAY IN ORDINARY TIME

Prayer

The psalmist writes, "You open wide your hand and satisfy the desire of every living thing" (Ps 145:16). Loving God, give us grateful hearts to receive the gifts you share, trusting you provide us with all we need. In a special way, open our hearts to the gift of yourself in this Eucharist so that we might know you more fully, love you more deeply, and serve you more faithfully in all we do. **Amen.**

SIXTEENTH SUNDAY IN ORDINARY TIME

Our psalmist today reminds us that those who do justice will live in the presence of the Lord. Calling to mind the times we have failed to act with justice and righteousness, we ask for the Lord's pardon and peace . . .

Prayer

Welcoming God, Abraham invited your messengers into his tent and was rewarded with a son. Jesus went to Martha's home, where she and Mary learned from you. Give us the wisdom to be hospitable to strangers, knowing that Christ is present in all we meet. With open hearts, we pray. **Amen**.

Gospel **Luke 10:38-42**

Jesus entered a village where a woman whose name was Martha welcomed him. She had a sister named Mary who sat beside the Lord at his feet listening to him speak. Martha, burdened with much serving, came to him and said, "Lord, do you not care that my sister has left me by myself to do the serving? Tell her to help me." The Lord said to her in reply, "Martha, Martha, you are anxious and worried about many things. There is need of only one thing. Mary has chosen the better part and it will not be taken from her."

Brief Silence

For Reflection

Some scholars think today's gospel passage is not about the tension between active and contemplative living, but about conflicts surrounding women's exercise of their ministries in the early church. Some people favored women evangelizers and teachers like Prisca (Acts 18:26), Euodia and Syntyche (Phil 4:2); women prophets like Philip's four daughters (Acts 21:9); and women heads of house churches, like Nympha (Col 4:15), Mary (Acts 12:12), Lydia (Acts 16:40), and Prisca (Rom 16:3; 1 Cor 16:19). Others, however, argued that a woman's place was in the home and that speaking and ministering in the public sphere belonged to the men (e.g., 1 Cor 14:34-35; 1 Tim 2:11-12). Luke takes the latter position, giving it validity by placing approval of the silent Mary on Jesus's lips.

There was never any question in the early church about women becoming disciples. Both Martha and Mary welcomed Jesus and the word he spoke (vv. 38-39). The controversy swirled around what women would do with what they learned while sitting at Jesus's feet. The answer Luke gave was quite understandable for his time. Today's gospel invites us to reflect on what answer Jesus might give today to the question of a woman's place in the ministries of the church.

✦ Do you identify more with Martha or with Mary? How do Jesus's words to Martha make you feel? How are they reassuring? How are they an invitation to growth?

Brief Silence

Prayer

The psalmist writes, "You open wide your hand and satisfy the desire of every living thing" (Ps 145:16). Loving God, give us grateful hearts to receive the gifts you share, trusting you provide us with all we need. In a special way, open our hearts to the gift of yourself in this Eucharist so that we might know you more fully, love you more deeply, and serve you more faithfully in all we do. **Amen.**

SEVENTEENTH SUNDAY IN ORDINARY TIME

When we call for help the Lord answers us. Let us turn our hearts to the Lord and ask for his mercy . . .

Prayer

Most generous God, you have gifted us with all we have, and still you tell us that all we need to do is ask and we shall receive. May we daily turn to you, asking for your forgiveness and trusting that you will answer our call. Confident in your unfailing love, we pray. **Amen**.

Gospel **Luke 11:1-13**

Jesus was praying in a certain place, and when he had finished, one of his disciples said to him, "Lord, teach us to pray just as John taught his disciples." He said to them, "When you pray, say: / Father, hallowed be your name, / your kingdom come. / Give us each day our daily bread / and forgive us our sins / for we ourselves forgive everyone in debt to us, / and do not subject us to the final test."

And he said to them, "Suppose one of you has a friend to whom he goes at midnight and says, 'Friend, lend me three loaves of bread, for a friend of mine has arrived at my house from a journey and I have nothing to offer him,' and he says in reply from within, 'Do not bother me; the door has already been locked and my children and I are already in bed. I cannot get up to give you anything.' I tell you, if he does not get up to give the visitor the loaves because of their friendship, he will get up to give him whatever he needs because of his persistence.

"And I tell you, ask and you will receive; seek and you will find; knock and the door will be opened to you. For everyone who asks, receives; and the one who seeks, finds; and to the one who knocks, the door will be opened. What father among you would hand his son a snake when he asks for a fish? Or hand him a scorpion when he asks for an egg? If you then, who are wicked, know how to give good gifts to your children, how much more will the Father in heaven give the Holy Spirit to those who ask him?"

Brief Silence

For Reflection

Sometimes we feel like we have to bargain with God to receive his favors. In the gospel today, Jesus tells a parable, then several sayings, to convey how greatly God wants to shower us with what is good.

Jesus tells a parable about a person who has a special need late at night, after a guest arrives unexpectedly. He goes to his neighbor to ask for bread to serve to the guest. The motive ascribed to the friend making the request in verse 8, *anaideia*, is often rendered "persistence." But the Greek word is more accurately translated "shamelessness." The sense is that the sleeping friend responds to the request for bread to avoid the shame of refusing the help.

The sayings that follow the parable reinforce its meaning, elaborating that God stands ready and eager to open the door to whoever knocks and to give whatever we ask, just as parents desire to give good gifts to their children.

The gospel challenges the idea that God sends suffering to test or challenge or strengthen us and insists that God desires only good for us. We do not have to badger God or bargain with God to give us good things.

✦ Jesus teaches us to call God our Father, but fatherhood is far from the only human image that teaches us about God. What images for God speak most to you at this point in your faith journey?

Brief Silence

SEVENTEENTH SUNDAY IN ORDINARY TIME

Prayer

The psalmist writes, "You open wide your hand and satisfy the desire of every living thing" (Ps 145:16). Loving God, give us grateful hearts to receive the gifts you share, trusting you provide us with all we need. In a special way, open our hearts to the gift of yourself in this Eucharist so that we might know you more fully, love you more deeply, and serve you more faithfully in all we do. **Amen.**

EIGHTEENTH SUNDAY IN ORDINARY TIME

Remembering our need for the Lord's mercy, we come before him asking that he teach us wisdom of heart . . .

Prayer

Giver of all gifts, you are so generous with us, yet we do not acknowledge your goodness. Too often we find ourselves concerned about what is fair, or what is owed us. May we hear your voice and soften our hearts, so that we may live more fully for you. We ask this through Christ, our Lord. **Amen**.

Gospel **Luke 12:13-21**

Someone in the crowd said to Jesus, "Teacher, tell my brother to share the inheritance with me." He replied to him, "Friend, who appointed me as your judge and arbitrator?" Then he said to the crowd, "Take care to guard against all greed, for though one may be rich, one's life does not consist of possessions."

Then he told them a parable. "There was a rich man whose land produced a bountiful harvest. He asked himself, 'What shall I do, for I do not have space to store my harvest?' And he said, 'This is what I shall do: I shall tear down my barns and build larger ones. There I shall store all my grain and other goods and I shall say to myself, "Now as for you, you have so many good things stored up for many years, rest, eat, drink, be merry!"' But God said to him, 'You fool, this night your life will be demanded of you; and the things you have prepared, to whom will they belong?' Thus will it be for all who store up treasure for themselves but are not rich in what matters to God."

Brief Silence

For Reflection

The gospel today shows us in parable form what the "greed that is idolatry" looks like. The rich man's self-centered plan for stockpiling and spending for his own enjoyment is interrupted by a startling apparition by God. "You fool," comes the accusation, everything belongs to God; even life itself is given to us on loan.

The parable also hints at how the miserly man will meet his end. If Jesus was addressing this parable to poor peasants, whose backbreaking labor only increased the riches of the landowner, the answer to the question of ownership would have a different ring. Wouldn't the land and its fruits, which come from their toil, belong to them? Is it the peasant workers who, in an uprising, are demanding the life of the rich man?

The parable cuts two ways: to those who are blessed with abundance, hard questions are posed about legitimate use, greediness, and just distribution of resources for the common good. To those on the underside of privilege, there is encouragement to take action to unmask vicious greed and to engage in efforts to bring about economic justice, while heeding an implicit warning that violence and killing are futile means for achieving just ends.

✦ When you remember that your life will come to an end, does it make you want to make any changes to how you are spending your limited time on earth?

Brief Silence

Prayer

The psalmist writes, "You open wide your hand and satisfy the desire of every living thing" (Ps 145:16). Loving God, give us grateful hearts to receive the gifts you share, trusting you provide us with all we need. In a special way, open our hearts to the gift of yourself in this Eucharist so that we might know you more fully, love you more deeply, and serve you more faithfully in all we do. **Amen.**

NINETEENTH SUNDAY IN ORDINARY TIME

In the gospel today, Jesus tells us not to be afraid but to prepare for his coming. Calling to mind the times we have failed to ready our hearts for him, we ask for his pardon and peace . . .

Prayer

God of hope, as our ancestors trusted in you and were rewarded, we now choose also to trust. We have been given much: may we now return to you the gifts you have bestowed upon us, believing that you have chosen us to be your own. In Jesus's name we pray. **Amen**.

Gospel **Luke 12:32-48 (or Luke 12:35-40)**

Jesus said to his disciples: "Do not be afraid any longer, little flock, for your Father is pleased to give you the kingdom. Sell your belongings and give alms. Provide money bags for yourselves that do not wear out, an inexhaustible treasure in heaven that no thief can reach nor moth destroy. For where your treasure is, there also will your heart be.

"Gird your loins and light your lamps and be like servants who await their master's return from a wedding, ready to open immediately when he comes and knocks. Blessed are those servants whom the master finds vigilant on his arrival. Amen, I say to you, he will gird himself, have them recline at table, and proceed to wait on them. And should he come in the second or third watch and find them prepared in this way, blessed are those servants. Be sure of this: if the master of the house had known the hour when the thief was coming, he would not have let his house be broken into. You also must be prepared, for at an hour you do not expect, the Son of Man will come."

Then Peter said, "Lord, is this parable meant for us or for everyone?" And the Lord replied, "Who, then, is the faithful and prudent steward whom the master will put in charge of his servants to distribute the food allowance at the proper time? Blessed is that servant whom his master on arrival finds doing so. Truly, I say to you, the master will put the servant in charge of all his property. But if that servant says to himself, 'My master is delayed in coming,' and begins to beat the menservants and the maidservants, to eat and drink and get drunk, then that servant's master will come on an unexpected day and at an unknown hour and will punish the servant severely and assign him a place with the unfaithful. That servant who knew his master's will but did not make preparations nor act in accord with his will shall be beaten severely; and the servant who was ignorant of his master's will but acted in a way deserving of a severe beating shall be beaten only lightly. Much will be required of the person entrusted with much, and still more will be demanded of the person entrusted with more."

Brief Silence

For Reflection

Today's gospel outlines how one becomes disposed to hear, to know, and to act on God's will. First, one must let go of fear to be able to receive the gift of God's kingdom. This is God's great joy: to find us unafraid and delighting in this indescribable gift. Obedience out of fear of a punishing God has no place among Jesus's followers. Rather, obedience is the single-hearted response in faith to the One who is love incarnate and who frees us to love in like manner.

Freeing the heart from attachment to anything but God's love and God's realm is the next step in obedience. Selling belongings and giving alms ensures that possessions do not become the treasure that grips the heart. Also needed is a sharpening of the senses, watching intently for all signs of divine presence and directives, through vigilance in prayer and attentiveness to the hungers of our world. Finally, when the master becomes the servant, there is a dismantling of systems wherein some are masters and others servants. The meaning of this parable will become clear at the Last Supper, where it will be enacted by Jesus himself when he washes his disciples' feet.

✦ How is your faith doing in the middle of this long stretch of Ordinary Time? How could you re-commit to the watchful vigilance that Jesus advises in this gospel?

Brief Silence

Prayer

The psalmist writes, "You open wide your hand and satisfy the desire of every living thing" (Ps 145:16). Loving God, give us grateful hearts to receive the gifts you share, trusting you provide us with all we need. In a special way, open our hearts to the gift of yourself in this Eucharist so that we might know you more fully, love you more deeply, and serve you more faithfully in all we do. **Amen.**

ASSUMPTION OF THE BLESSED VIRGIN MARY

We celebrate the Assumption of the Blessed Virgin Mary, born without sin and assumed into heaven. Mary, Mother of the Church and Mother of God, calls us always to her Son. Let us be mindful of the times we have failed to follow him . . .

Prayer

Holy Mary, with you we lift our voices in praise of God, and our spirits also rejoice. The Almighty has done good things for all of humanity through your "yes," and we are truly filled with joy. May we strive to be more like you in all we do. Mother of God, pray for us sinners. **Amen**.

Gospel **Luke 1:39-56; At the Mass during the Day**

Mary set out and traveled to the hill country in haste to a town of Judah, where she entered the house of Zechariah and greeted Elizabeth. When Elizabeth heard Mary's greeting, the infant leaped in her womb, and Elizabeth, filled with the Holy Spirit, cried out in a loud voice and said, "Blessed are you among women, and blessed is the fruit of your womb. And how does this happen to me, that the mother of my Lord should come to me? For at the moment the sound of your greeting reached my ears, the infant in my womb leaped for joy. Blessed are you who believed that what was spoken to you by the Lord would be fulfilled."

And Mary said: / "My soul proclaims the greatness of the Lord; / my spirit rejoices in God my Savior / for he has looked with favor on his lowly servant. / From this day all generations will call me blessed: / the Almighty has done great things for me, / and holy is his Name. / He has mercy on those who fear him / in every generation. / He has shown the strength of his arm, / and has scattered the proud in their conceit. / He has cast down the mighty from their thrones, / and has lifted up the lowly. / He has filled the hungry with good things, / and the rich he has sent away empty. / He has come to the help of his servant Israel / for he has remembered his promise of mercy, / the promise he made to our fathers, / to Abraham and his children forever."

Mary remained with her about three months and then returned to her home.

Brief Silence

For Reflection

Today's feast underscores the importance of bodiliness, declaring that Mary, "having completed the course of her earthly life, was assumed body and soul into heavenly glory" (Pope Pius XII, *Munificentissimus Deus*).

In today's gospel, there is an emphasis on the holiness of the body as a vehicle for the saving life God brings to birth. Both Elizabeth and Mary exemplify an incarnational spirituality, whereby God's action in this world is known through bodiliness. With the infant in her womb leaping for joy, Elizabeth is filled with the Spirit and she pronounces a blessing on Mary and on the child she carries in her body. Mary, in turn, proclaims God's greatness with her whole being (the Greek word *psyche* in verse 46, usually translated "soul," is not a separate part of the human, as opposed to the body, but rather refers to the whole self in all its vitality). Mary prophesies a new world in which there are no longer hungry or exploited bodies.

✦ Mary and Elizabeth witness God's work together. They share what they have experienced and find affirmation of their own experiences in each other's. In so doing, they model Christian community. Who is the Elizabeth to your Mary (or vice versa)? With whom do you walk on your spiritual journey?

Brief Silence

Prayer

ASSUMPTION OF THE BLESSED VIRGIN MARY

The psalmist writes, “You open wide your hand and satisfy the desire of every living thing” (Ps 145:16). Loving God, give us grateful hearts to receive the gifts you share, trusting you provide us with all we need. In a special way, open our hearts to the gift of yourself in this Eucharist so that we might know you more fully, love you more deeply, and serve you more faithfully in all we do. **Amen.**

TWENTIETH SUNDAY IN ORDINARY TIME

Today's psalm reminds us that God always come to our aid. For those times when we have strayed from God our help, we seek his pardon and peace . . .

Prayer

Lord Jesus Christ, you came to set the world on fire, and to free us from our sinfulness. In our time of need, we turn to you: Lord, come to our aid! May we not grow weary, but fix our eyes on you and take courage, knowing of your great love for us. With trust in you, we pray. **Amen**.

Gospel **Luke 12:49-53**

Jesus said to his disciples: "I have come to set the earth on fire, and how I wish it were already blazing! There is a baptism with which I must be baptized, and how great is my anguish until it is accomplished! Do you think that I have come to establish peace on the earth? No, I tell you, but rather division. From now on a household of five will be divided, three against two and two against three; a father will be divided against his son and a son against his father, a mother against her daughter and a daughter against her mother, a mother-in-law against her daughter-in-law and a daughter-in-law against her mother-in-law."

Brief Silence

For Reflection

We see a kind of tug-of-war in the first reading. Some heed the prophet's words and welcome his warning, while others resist the threat to their power, privilege, and status that Jeremiah's message poses. Jesus speaks of the same kind of divided reaction that his ministry provokes. As he ignites in his followers a vision of justice, peace, and well-being for all, some welcome it. Others resist the burning away of their comforts and privileges that Jesus's way of transformation demands.

Jesus warns his followers not to be surprised if his message provokes conflict and division. The way toward genuine peace is not a gentle, easy road. It's a path that entails struggle. Injustice does not die without heavy resistance. Those who embark on Jesus's way, however, are empowered by their baptism. Baptism brings both refreshment and joy from being washed of sin, as well as an induction into a difficult, lifelong burning away of anything within that stands opposed to the gospel. Inflamed with the power of the Spirit, those baptized in Christ are empowered to continue his mission of healing divisions, as diverse hearts and minds are fused into one in the furnace of Christ's love.

✦ While we are not necessarily called to take on unnecessary suffering, is there a way you could take on a bit of someone else's burden? How might you be called to relieve the suffering of someone else?

Brief Silence

Prayer

The psalmist writes, "You open wide your hand and satisfy the desire of every living thing" (Ps 145:16). Loving God, give us grateful hearts to receive the gifts you share, trusting you provide us with all we need. In a special way, open our hearts to the gift of yourself in this Eucharist so that we might know you more fully, love you more deeply, and serve you more faithfully in all we do. **Amen.**

TWENTY-FIRST SUNDAY IN ORDINARY TIME

Today, Saint Paul tells us that God addresses us as his children. Aware that he longs to receive us as his own, let us seek God's pardon for those times we have turned away from him . . .

Prayer

God of our salvation, Jesus reminds us that we must pass through the narrow gate. We ask for strength and steadfast endurance in times of trial, so that we may obtain righteousness, glorify you, and announce your good news to all the world. In your holy name we pray. **Amen.**

Gospel **Luke 13:22-30**

Jesus passed through towns and villages, teaching as he went and making his way to Jerusalem. Someone asked him, "Lord, will only a few people be saved?" He answered them, "Strive to enter through the narrow gate, for many, I tell you, will attempt to enter but will not be strong enough. After the master of the house has arisen and locked the door, then will you stand outside knocking and saying, 'Lord, open the door for us.' He will say to you in reply, 'I do not know where you are from.' And you will say, 'We ate and drank in your company and you taught in our streets.' Then he will say to you, 'I do not know where you are from. Depart from me, all you evildoers!' And there will be wailing and grinding of teeth when you see Abraham, Isaac, and Jacob and all the prophets in the kingdom of God and you yourselves cast out. And people will come from the east and the west and from the north and the south and will recline at table in the kingdom of God. For behold, some are last who will be first, and some are first who will be last."

Brief Silence

For Reflection

Today's gospel starts with someone asking Jesus, "Will only a few people be saved?" Jesus advises that one must "strive to enter through the narrow gate." The verb *agōnizomai*, "strive," is used to describe athletic training. Just as an athlete must gradually build up strength through daily exercise, so spiritual fitness takes consistent effort and training. Jesus notes that many who attempt to enter will not be strong enough.

In the gospel Jesus speaks about what can happen to those who do not put any effort into "working out" spiritually. When the final moment comes, they will be on the outside pleading to get in, thinking that just having been present where Jesus was teaching would be enough; it is like someone who goes to the gym but only watches other people go through their paces. It will be too late then to start training. Jesus returns to the original question and, echoing the first reading from Isaiah, envisions masses of people from all directions who will be included among those saved. We may be surprised by who gets there first.

✦ God is more generous and merciful than we could ever hope to comprehend. What helps you remember the vastness of God's love?

Brief Silence

Prayer

The psalmist writes, "You open wide your hand and satisfy the desire of every living thing" (Ps 145:16). Loving God, give us grateful hearts to receive the gifts you share, trusting you provide us with all we need. In a special way, open our hearts to the gift of yourself in this Eucharist so that we might know you more fully, love you more deeply, and serve you more faithfully in all we do. **Amen.**

TWENTY-SECOND SUNDAY IN ORDINARY TIME

Today's reading from Sirach urges us to conduct ourselves with humility and wisdom. For those times that we have allowed sin to take us beyond what is good, we turn to Christ, seeking his forgiveness . . .

Prayer

O God, you are good and forgiving, and in your love, we rejoice. Jesus humbled himself as a servant: teach us to be more humble, putting others before ourselves, that the world might be reminded that the last shall be first, and that it is in giving that we shall receive. In humility, we pray. **Amen**.

Gospel **Luke 14:1, 7-14**

On a sabbath Jesus went to dine at the home of one of the leading Pharisees, and the people there were observing him carefully.

He told a parable to those who had been invited, noticing how they were choosing the places of honor at the table. "When you are invited by someone to a wedding banquet, do not recline at table in the place of honor. A more distinguished guest than you may have been invited by him, and the host who invited both of you may approach you and say, 'Give your place to this man,' and then you would proceed with embarrassment to take the lowest place. Rather, when you are invited, go and take the lowest place so that when the host comes to you he may say, 'My friend, move up to a higher position.' Then you will enjoy the esteem of your companions at the table. For everyone who exalts himself will be humbled, but the one who humbles himself will be exalted." Then he said to the host who invited him, "When you hold a lunch or a dinner, do not invite your friends or your brothers or your relatives or your wealthy neighbors, in case they may invite you back and you have repayment. Rather, when you hold a banquet, invite the poor, the crippled, the lame, the blind; blessed indeed will you be because of their inability to repay you. For you will be repaid at the resurrection of the righteous."

Brief Silence

For Reflection

In the gospel, Jesus gives concrete examples of how one can go about growing in humility. He is at a dinner hosted by a leading Pharisee. Jesus first addresses the invited guests about choosing places at the table. The setting presumes that these are people with a certain measure of power and prestige. Banquets were occasions for people to enhance their social standing and Jesus describes how guests would compete for honor. The way to gain the most honor, he says, is actually to take the lowest place.

Jesus then turns his attention to the host of the dinner and talks about how to formulate a guest list. From this angle, he again prods his hearers to break out of the strictures of likes eating with likes. The conversations at tables of the like-minded serve only to reinforce their own views, and the circle tightens as they reciprocate invitations to one another. Instead, Jesus proposes to the host, invite those unlike yourself, those with whom no one wants to associate. From a stance of humility, such a host recognizes the bond shared through common humanity that is stronger than differences in abilities or social positions.

✦ What does hospitality mean to you? How might God be calling you to exceed a secular definition of this term and lean into truly radical and self-giving hospitality?

Brief Silence

Prayer

The psalmist writes, "You open wide your hand and satisfy the desire of every living thing" (Ps 145:16). Loving God, give us grateful hearts to receive the gifts you share, trusting you provide us with all we need. In a special way, open our hearts to the gift of yourself in this Eucharist so that we might know you more fully, love you more deeply, and serve you more faithfully in all we do. **Amen.**

TWENTY-THIRD SUNDAY IN ORDINARY TIME

Today's psalm reminds us that God is our refuge. Let us turn to him as we seek his pardon for those times that we have strayed from his care . . .

Prayer

God of all wisdom, in our haste and our pride, we often think we can "go it on our own." But Jesus reminds us that, as his disciples, we each must carry our own cross. Teach us your ways, that we may gain your wisdom and work toward building your kingdom. We ask this through Christ, our Lord. **Amen**.

Gospel **Luke 14:25-33**

Great crowds were traveling with Jesus, and he turned and addressed them, "If anyone comes to me without hating his father and mother, wife and children, brothers and sisters, and even his own life, he cannot be my disciple. Whoever does not carry his own cross and come after me cannot be my disciple. Which of you wishing to construct a tower does not first sit down and calculate the cost to see if there is enough for its completion? Otherwise, after laying the foundation and finding himself unable to finish the work the onlookers should laugh at him and say, 'This one began to build but did not have the resources to finish.' Or what king marching into battle would not first sit down and decide whether with ten thousand troops he can successfully oppose another king advancing upon him with twenty thousand troops? But if not, while he is still far away, he will send a delegation to ask for peace terms. In the same way, anyone of you who does not renounce all his possessions cannot be my disciple."

Brief Silence

For Reflection

The saying about hating one's own family members is jolting to our ears, as it was to Jesus's first followers. In Jesus's time, people did not conceive of themselves as individuals but derived their identity and social standing from their family, clan, village, and religious group. It would be unimaginable to cut oneself off from family; this would be tantamount to losing life itself.

Looking at other passages in the Gospel of Luke, we see that Jesus himself does not renounce his family. Unlike Mark (3:31-35), Luke (8:21) leaves open the possibility that Jesus's blood kin can also be disciples. In fact, Luke portrays Jesus's mother as one who faithfully hears the word of God and obeys; and in the story of Pentecost (Acts 1:14), Luke notes that Jesus's mother and siblings are among the disciples in the Upper Room. What Jesus asks, however, is that a disciple be willing to embrace as kin others who are not related by blood. Disciples must act as brother and sister toward those who are different, whether by physical ability or any other status marker.

✦ What crosses are you carrying these days? How can your community support you in bearing them?

Brief Silence

Prayer

The psalmist writes, "You open wide your hand and satisfy the desire of every living thing" (Ps 145:16). Loving God, give us grateful hearts to receive the gifts you share, trusting you provide us with all we need. In a special way, open our hearts to the gift of yourself in this Eucharist so that we might know you more fully, love you more deeply, and serve you more faithfully in all we do. **Amen.**

THE EXALTATION OF THE HOLY CROSS

The Letter to the Philippians assures us that Christ emptied himself for our sake. Recalling those times when we have strayed from him, let us seek his pardon and peace . . .

Prayer

Loving God, you sent your Son into the world that all might believe in him and have eternal life. As Jesus humbled himself by his death on the cross, may we also learn greater humility in our day-to-day interactions with others, and so glorify you by our lives. In Jesus's name we pray. **Amen**.

Gospel **John 3:13-17**

Jesus said to Nicodemus: "No one has gone up to heaven except the one who has come down from heaven, the Son of Man. And just as Moses lifted up the serpent in the desert, so must the Son of Man be lifted up, so that everyone who believes in him may have eternal life."

For God so loved the world that he gave his only Son, so that he who believes in him might not perish but might have eternal life. For God did not send his Son into the world to condemn the world, but that the world might be saved through him.

Brief Silence

For Reflection

In the *Saint John's Bible* depiction of the crucifixion scene, both cross and Christ are pure gold, the total revelation of God's very self, shown against a cosmic background—this is an event that resounds through all time and space. By the love of Christ outpoured, the atrocity of the crucifixion becomes something profoundly beautiful. The cross is no longer simply an instrument of death but has become the means by which we are given abundant life.

In this courageous act of love, we find reason for hope and a decisive direction for our own life. We have no reason to fear either life or death, as God's redeeming love is enough for us. As was the case with the serpent in the desert, "lifted up" for all in search of healing to look upon, we are offered wholeness and redemption in gazing upon the cross. However, in turning to the cross, we also must recognize Jesus's destiny as our own. We, too, must be "lifted up" with Christ, born from above in baptism and thus united with him in his death and resurrection. If we love as Christ loves, we will not escape our own crosses.

✦ What emotional reaction do you have to the crucifixion story? It might range from horror at Jesus's suffering to sorrow for your own sins to hope in the transformation Jesus offers. None of these is wrong, and we might cycle through them as we move through our journey with Christ.

Brief Silence

Prayer

The psalmist writes, "You open wide your hand and satisfy the desire of every living thing" (Ps 145:16). Loving God, give us grateful hearts to receive the gifts you share, trusting you provide us with all we need. In a special way, open our hearts to the gift of yourself in this Eucharist so that we might know you more fully, love you more deeply, and serve you more faithfully in all we do. **Amen.**

TWENTY-FIFTH SUNDAY IN ORDINARY TIME

In our gospel today, Jesus warns against serving anyone other than God as our master. Calling to mind the times we have allowed sin to master our lives, we ask for his pardon and peace . . .

Prayer

Lord, our God, you know us and our failings, and yet you love us unconditionally. We praise you for raising up those in poverty, for we know ourselves to be poor in your sight. You have trusted us with much: may we be found worthy of that trust. We ask this in the name of Jesus. **Amen**.

Gospel **Luke 16:1-13 (or Luke 16:10-13)**

Jesus said to his disciples, "A rich man had a steward who was reported to him for squandering his property. He summoned him and said, 'What is this I hear about you? Prepare a full account of your stewardship, because you can no longer be my steward.' The steward said to himself, 'What shall I do, now that my master is taking the position of steward away from me? I am not strong enough to dig and I am ashamed to beg. I know what I shall do so that, when I am removed from the stewardship, they may welcome me into their homes.' He called in his master's debtors one by one. To the first he said, 'How much do you owe my master?' He replied, 'One hundred measures of olive oil.' He said to him, 'Here is your promissory note. Sit down and quickly write one for fifty.' Then to another the steward said, 'And you, how much do you owe?' He replied, 'One hundred kors of wheat.' The steward said to him, 'Here is your promissory note; write one for eighty.' And the master commended that dishonest steward for acting prudently.

"For the children of this world are more prudent in dealing with their own generation than are the children of light. I tell you, make friends for yourselves with dishonest wealth, so that when it fails, you will be welcomed into eternal dwellings. The person who is trustworthy in very small matters is also trustworthy in great ones; and the person who is dishonest in very small matters is also dishonest in great ones. If, therefore, you are not trustworthy with dishonest wealth, who will trust you with true wealth? If you are not trustworthy with what belongs to another, who will give you what is yours? No servant can serve two masters. He will either hate one and love the other, or be devoted to one and despise the other. You cannot serve both God and mammon."

Brief Silence

For Reflection

Things aren't as simple as they used to be—or so it seems! Perhaps there never really was a time when issues were clear-cut and moral decisions were easy.

The parable in today's gospel is itself so complex that the only thing biblical scholars agree on is that it poses more questions than it answers, and no interpretation fully answers all of them. How can a dishonest steward be praised by his master? Who is the master? Jesus? The rich man? Is the parable about lost honor or lost income? What is the economic system presumed in the story? Does it concern usury? Or the steward's commission? What does "squandering" signify? Is the charge true or false? Who are the debtors? Is the master a sympathetic character or a villain? Is the steward someone to be emulated or is he designed to give us a chuckle?

One possibility for this Sunday is not to try to settle the interpretation of the gospel parable but to look instead at the underlying values and attitudes that the readings propose, which orient us toward what we must do in order to be able to make good moral decisions in complex situations.

✦ What in your life threatens to be "mammon," a false object of devotion? What things do you spend your time, attention, and money on? Do they align with your true values?

TWENTY-FIFTH SUNDAY IN ORDINARY TIME

Brief Silence

Prayer

The psalmist writes, "You open wide your hand and satisfy the desire of every living thing" (Ps 145:16). Loving God, give us grateful hearts to receive the gifts you share, trusting you provide us with all we need. In a special way, open our hearts to the gift of yourself in this Eucharist so that we might know you more fully, love you more deeply, and serve you more faithfully in all we do. **Amen.**

TWENTY-SIXTH SUNDAY IN ORDINARY TIME

The Lord warns us not to be complacent with our love. Calling to mind the times we have failed to love as Christ has called us, we ask for his pardon and peace . . .

Prayer

God of the poor and the marginalized, too often we overlook—or even disdain—those who are less fortunate than we are. But blessed are you, who hear the cries of those in need! May we learn to love as you love, and to see the world through Jesus's eyes. In humility, we pray. **Amen**.

Gospel **Luke 16:19-31**

Jesus said to the Pharisees: "There was a rich man who dressed in purple garments and fine linen and dined sumptuously each day. And lying at his door was a poor man named Lazarus, covered with sores, who would gladly have eaten his fill of the scraps that fell from the rich man's table. Dogs even used to come and lick his sores. When the poor man died, he was carried away by angels to the bosom of Abraham. The rich man also died and was buried, and from the netherworld, where he was in torment, he raised his eyes and saw Abraham far off and Lazarus at his side. And he cried out, 'Father Abraham, have pity on me. Send Lazarus to dip the tip of his finger in water and cool my tongue for I am suffering torment in these flames.' Abraham replied, 'My child, remember that you received what was good during your lifetime while Lazarus likewise received what was bad; but now he is comforted here, whereas you are tormented. Moreover, between us and you a great chasm is established to prevent anyone from crossing who might wish to go from our side to yours or from your side to ours.'

He said, 'Then I beg you, father, send him to my father's house, for I have five brothers, so that he may warn them, lest they too come to this place of torment.' But Abraham replied, 'They have Moses and the prophets. Let them listen to them.' He said, 'Oh no, father Abraham, but if someone from the dead goes to them, they will repent.' Then Abraham said, 'If they will not listen to Moses and the prophets, neither will they be persuaded if someone should rise from the dead.'"

Brief Silence

For Reflection

In today's gospel reading, Jesus tells a story of a rich man who steps over a destitute brother who is lying right at his doorstep. The rich man pays no attention to the poor man, Lazarus, until he needs something from him. From his tormented place in the afterlife, the rich man wants Lazarus to bring him the relief of cool water. When Abraham replies that this is impossible, then the rich man asks Abraham to send Lazarus to warn his brothers.

Abraham does not grant the rich man either request. The vast differences between him and Lazarus could have been bridged during the rich man's lifetime, but he chose not to respond to his brother. He had everything he needed from Moses and the prophets to know what to do.

Moses, the prophets, and Jesus have given us all we need to know to bridge the chasm between rich and poor in this life. We begin by recognizing those made poor not as an abstraction but as real persons who have names, most of whom are women and children, who are sister and brother to us. From there, the gap is bridgeable.

✦ Who is a Lazarus in your life? What needs in others might you be overlooking as you go about your day-to-day busyness? What luxuries do you find yourself indulging in regularly? Could you find a way to cut back on something to make more room for sharing your resources with others?

Brief Silence

TWENTY-SIXTH SUNDAY IN ORDINARY TIME

Prayer

The psalmist writes, "You open wide your hand and satisfy the desire of every living thing" (Ps 145:16). Loving God, give us grateful hearts to receive the gifts you share, trusting you provide us with all we need. In a special way, open our hearts to the gift of yourself in this Eucharist so that we might know you more fully, love you more deeply, and serve you more faithfully in all we do. **Amen.**

TWENTY-SEVENTH SUNDAY IN ORDINARY TIME

Our God calls us to confront destruction and violence before us and within our own hearts. Following his command, we call to mind our need for his mercy . . .

Prayer

Rock of our salvation, you are steadfast in your love for us, despite our lack of faith and our unbelief. May we hear and respond to your voice, that our hearts might be softened and our lives reflect the good gifts you have given us. Trusting in your promise, we pray to you, O Lord. **Amen**.

Gospel **Luke 17:5-10**

The apostles said to the Lord, "Increase our faith." The Lord replied, "If you have faith the size of a mustard seed, you would say to this mulberry tree, 'Be uprooted and planted in the sea,' and it would obey you.

"Who among you would say to your servant who has just come in from plowing or tending sheep in the field, 'Come here immediately and take your place at table'? Would he not rather say to him, 'Prepare something for me to eat. Put on your apron and wait on me while I eat and drink. You may eat and drink when I am finished'? Is he grateful to that servant because he did what was commanded? So should it be with you. When you have done all you have been commanded, say, 'We are unprofitable servants; we have done what we were obliged to do.'"

Brief Silence

For Reflection

The disciples in today's gospel want Jesus to fix things by giving them more faith. Jesus reassures them that they already have faith enough to transform what seems utterly immovable. A mulberry tree has a deep and extensive root system and is extremely difficult to uproot and replant. It is an apt image for deep-rooted systems of injustice and violence. A mustard seed, by contrast, is tiny, but spreads like wildfire, and is also nearly impossible to eradicate. Disciples who feel puny in the face of massive systems of injustice have all they need to do the transformative work toward fulfillment of Jesus's vision of the reign of God. Jesus encourages them by saying not only that they have all the faith they need but also that it is by their persistent, day-in, day-out service that the transformation of seemingly intractable systems comes about. Moreover, just as fieldwork and table service were simply what was required of a slave in Jesus's time, so faithful service on behalf of the gospel is what is expected of disciples.

✦ How do you respond to unanswered prayers? What helps you remember to be patient with God's timeline rather than imposing your own?

Brief Silence

Prayer

The psalmist writes, "You open wide your hand and satisfy the desire of every living thing" (Ps 145:16). Loving God, give us grateful hearts to receive the gifts you share, trusting you provide us with all we need. In a special way, open our hearts to the gift of yourself in this Eucharist so that we might know you more fully, love you more deeply, and serve you more faithfully in all we do. **Amen.**

TWENTY-EIGHTH SUNDAY IN ORDINARY TIME

In our gospel today, Jesus cleanses ten who have faith but only one returns in thanksgiving. Uniting our faith to our thanksgiving, we come before the Lord as we prepare our hearts to celebrate these mysteries . . .

Prayer

Almighty God, you have shown your glory and power to all the ends of the earth through countless miracles, including the healing of lepers. May we sing of your goodness today and all days, telling the world of your wondrous deeds. This we pray through our Lord, Jesus Christ. **Amen**.

Gospel **Luke 17:11-19**

As Jesus continued his journey to Jerusalem, he traveled through Samaria and Galilee. As he was entering a village, ten lepers met him. They stood at a distance from him and raised their voices, saying, "Jesus, Master! Have pity on us!" And when he saw them, he said, "Go show yourselves to the priests." As they were going they were cleansed. And one of them, realizing he had been healed, returned, glorifying God in a loud voice; and he fell at the feet of Jesus and thanked him. He was a Samaritan. Jesus said in reply, "Ten were cleansed, were they not? Where are the other nine? Has none but this foreigner returned to give thanks to God?" Then he said to him, "Stand up and go; your faith has saved you."

Brief Silence

For Reflection

The first reading and the gospel today tell stories of two different men afflicted with leprosy. Both are foreigners who nonetheless are healed by Israel's prophets, Elisha and Jesus. Both praise the God of Israel for their transformation.

In the gospel, the focus is on the way the one healed man turns around and loudly glorifies God, falling at Jesus's feet, thanking him. Perhaps this man's turning around was not only physical but interior as well; when he lets gratitude consume him, he turns around from any other cancers that eat at his spirit. Jesus affirms that this kind of faith, rooted in thankfulness, is the healing, saving power that enables him to go forward as a changed person, both in body and spirit.

Naaman struggles mightily to turn away from his stance of entitlement, from his attempts to buy healing, and to direct the manner in which it should occur. After his healing, Naaman still tries to pay for it, but Elisha will take nothing from him. All that God or Jesus desires in return is a heart shaped by saving gratitude for freely given grace that has the power to heal both the inner and outer self.

✦ Take a moment to join with the Samaritan leper in gratitude. What are you thankful for today?

Brief Silence

Prayer

The psalmist writes, "You open wide your hand and satisfy the desire of every living thing" (Ps 145:16). Loving God, give us grateful hearts to receive the gifts you share, trusting you provide us with all we need. In a special way, open our hearts to the gift of yourself in this Eucharist so that we might know you more fully, love you more deeply, and serve you more faithfully in all we do. **Amen.**

TWENTY-NINTH SUNDAY IN ORDINARY TIME

The Lord is our help who never slumbers or sleeps. Calling to mind the times we have failed to keep watch and have fallen into sin, we ask for his pardon and peace . . .

Prayer

Faithful God, we know that our help comes only from you, and we trust in your promise to protect us. May we be ever more steadfast in our prayers, believing that when we turn to you, you will answer our requests and come to our help. We ask this through Christ, our Lord. **Amen**.

Gospel **Luke 18:1-8**

Jesus told his disciples a parable about the necessity for them to pray always without becoming weary. He said, "There was a judge in a certain town who neither feared God nor respected any human being. And a widow in that town used to come to him and say, 'Render a just decision for me against my adversary.' For a long time the judge was unwilling, but eventually he thought, 'While it is true that I neither fear God nor respect any human being, because this widow keeps bothering me I shall deliver a just decision for her lest she finally come and strike me.'" The Lord said, "Pay attention to what the dishonest judge says. Will not God then secure the rights of his chosen ones who call out to him day and night? Will he be slow to answer them? I tell you, he will see to it that justice is done for them speedily. But when the Son of Man comes, will he find faith on earth?"

Brief Silence

For Reflection

The parable in today's gospel begins with the introduction of two characters: a judge who twice declares he has no fear of God and no respect for any human being, and a widow who comes to him over and over and over, day after day after day, insisting that justice be done.

The judge is impervious at first, but he finally relents because he is afraid she will haul off and give him a black eye! The verb *hypōpiazein* in verse 5 is often translated metaphorically as "wear me out," but it is a boxing term that literally means "to strike under the eye" (see also 1 Cor 9:26). It is a hilarious image: a supposedly powerful judge cowering in front of a seemingly powerless little widow.

The humorous vignette, however, conveys a very serious message: it is through persistence and tireless actions of nonviolent confrontation that justice is attained. More often than not, this happens through the repeated actions of seemingly inconsequential people, who never give up. Persistent prayer goes hand in hand with persistent action for justice.

✦ What is your prayer life like in this season of your faith journey? What do you wish it would look like? What are some prayer practices that have been fruitful at different stages of your life? How do you know when it is time to try a new one?

Brief Silence

Prayer

The psalmist writes, "You open wide your hand and satisfy the desire of every living thing" (Ps 145:16). Loving God, give us grateful hearts to receive the gifts you share, trusting you provide us with all we need. In a special way, open our hearts to the gift of yourself in this Eucharist so that we might know you more fully, love you more deeply, and serve you more faithfully in all we do. **Amen.**

THIRTIETH SUNDAY IN ORDINARY TIME

The Lord is a God of justice who hears those who cry out to him. Calling to mind our need for his mercy, we ask for his pardon and peace . . .

Prayer

God of justice and mercy, you hear the cries of the poor and the needy, and you hasten to their aid. We ask for your forgiveness, knowing that we fall short of serving and loving others as you have taught us. Grant us the humility to trust in your redeeming love. In your holy name we pray. **Amen**.

Gospel **Luke 18:9-14**

Jesus addressed this parable to those who were convinced of their own righteousness and despised everyone else. "Two people went up to the temple area to pray; one was a Pharisee and the other was a tax collector. The Pharisee took up his position and spoke this prayer to himself, 'O God, I thank you that I am not like the rest of humanity—greedy, dishonest, adulterous—or even like this tax collector. I fast twice a week, and I pay tithes on my whole income.' But the tax collector stood off at a distance and would not even raise his eyes to heaven but beat his breast and prayed, 'O God, be merciful to me a sinner.' I tell you, the latter went home justified, not the former; for whoever exalts himself will be humbled, and the one who humbles himself will be exalted."

Brief Silence

For Reflection

In Jesus's parable about a Pharisee and a tax collector, his original audience would have instinctively compared them, thinking the first to be admirable and the latter despicable. Pharisees were known for their piety. This one fasts and tithes above and beyond what is required. Surely these actions indicate that he is righteous. The Pharisee's prayer, however, indicates otherwise. He appears to have no need of God. The tax collector, meanwhile, beats his breast and prays simply, "O God, be merciful to me a sinner." Focusing on God, he prays for openness to divine mercy, which has the power to transform his sinfulness.

The end of the parable is startling: it is the tax collector who is in right relation. He is acutely aware of his utter dependence on God.

In truth, there's something of the Pharisee in us, as we so easily make comparisons, exalting ourselves by humiliating others. There's also something of the tax collector in us, who humbly recognizes his own weaknesses while opening himself to the Source of all mercy. The parable invites us to leave aside all comparisons and to seek oneness with the incomparably Merciful One. From this stance comes right relation with all.

✦ This gospel reminds us that God often subverts our expectations. Talk about a time when God surprised you, showing up in an unexpected person or place.

Brief Silence

Prayer

The psalmist writes, "You open wide your hand and satisfy the desire of every living thing" (Ps 145:16). Loving God, give us grateful hearts to receive the gifts you share, trusting you provide us with all we need. In a special way, open our hearts to the gift of yourself in this Eucharist so that we might know you more fully, love you more deeply, and serve you more faithfully in all we do. **Amen.**

Today we celebrate the Solemnity of All Saints, the faithful who have gone before us longing to see God's face. Remembering the times we have failed to live as God calls us, we ask for his pardon and peace . . .

Prayer

God of all blessings, we rejoice in the love you have shown us by sending your Son into the world. By imitating his example, we pray that we might someday be counted among the saints. Until that day, we consider ourselves blessed to be called your children. With thankful hearts, we pray. **Amen**.

Gospel **Matt 5:1-12a**

When Jesus saw the crowds, he went up the mountain, and after he had sat down, his disciples came to him. He began to teach them, saying: / "Blessed are the poor in spirit, / for theirs is the Kingdom of heaven. / Blessed are they who mourn, / for they will be comforted. / Blessed are the meek, / for they will inherit the land. / Blessed are they who hunger and thirst for righteousness, / for they will be satisfied. / Blessed are the merciful, / for they will be shown mercy. / Blessed are the clean of heart, / for they will see God. / Blessed are the peacemakers, / for they will be called children of God. / Blessed are they who are persecuted for the sake of righteousness, / for theirs is the Kingdom of heaven. / Blessed are you when they insult you and persecute you and utter every kind of evil against you falsely because of me. Rejoice and be glad, for your reward will be great in heaven."

Brief Silence

For Reflection

Some might accuse Catholic devotion to particular saints of distracting from the "one true mediatorship" of Jesus. Properly understood, the saints provide all the more reason to celebrate the love of Christ poured out for us. In a sense, the saints are like stained glass windows, filtering the light of Christ into a multitude of different colors, cultures, and centuries. The fact that there is a Saint Rose of Lima, a Saint Augustine of Hippo, and a Saint Ignatius of Loyola is itself a sign that the truth of Christ permeates all time and space—praise be to God!

The saints remind us that we, too, can share in this same grace of God. Every saint (save Mary) is a redeemed sinner, made whole in God's grace. Jesus spoke in the revelations to Saint Faustina, "There is no misery that could be a match for My mercy." We are offered the grace to be saints most clearly in the sacraments, where God meets us personally and profoundly. If we trust in God's love, by which we are truly *blessed now*, we know that we too will inherit the kingdom.

✦ Which of the beatitudes is most challenging for you right now? How might God be using it as an invitation to growth?

Brief Silence

Prayer

The psalmist writes, "You open wide your hand and satisfy the desire of every living thing" (Ps 145:16). Loving God, give us grateful hearts to receive the gifts you share, trusting you provide us with all we need. In a special way, open our hearts to the gift of yourself in this Eucharist so that we might know you more fully, love you more deeply, and serve you more faithfully in all we do. **Amen.**

THE COMMEMORATION OF ALL THE FAITHFUL DEPARTED (ALL SOULS' DAY)

As we pray for the souls of our faithful departed, we pray that we might learn to live with greater love as we ask for God's pardon and peace . . .

Prayer

Lord Jesus Christ, you have said that all who believe in you will never die, but will have eternal life. We trust in this promise and believe that we shall someday see you face-to-face. May those who have gone before us rest in your loving embrace. In your holy name we pray. **Amen**.

Gospel **John 6:37-40**

Jesus said to the crowds: "Everything that the Father gives me will come to me, and I will not reject anyone who comes to me, because I came down from heaven not to do my own will but the will of the one who sent me. And this is the will of the one who sent me, that I should not lose anything of what he gave me, but that I should raise it on the last day. For this is the will of my Father, that everyone who sees the Son and believes in him may have eternal life, and I shall raise him on the last day."

Brief Silence

Other gospel options for November 2:

Matthew 5:1-12a / Matthew 11:25-30 / Matthew 25:31-46 / Luke 7:11-17 / Luke 23:44-46, 50, 52-53; 24:1-6a / Luke 24:13-16, 28-35 / John 5:24-29 / John 6:51-58 / John 11:17-27 / John 11:32-45 / John 14:1-6

For Reflection

Anyone who knows the loss of a loved one knows the seeming finality of death, of saying goodbye to someone they held dear. That pain is real, and nothing can reverse that loss. Yet the first reading from Wisdom says it is only to the "foolish" that the just seem to be dead. Is it foolish to cling to hope that God would indeed raise the just? If we can recognize the evil of death when we see it, shall we not also see goodness? Faith can be difficult when reality seems to show anything but God's love and presence. We cling to the cross of Christ at the darkest times, when all else seems lost, because nothing else will hold. *Ave Crux, spes unica*—hail the cross, our only hope!

Jesus promises in the gospel that all who come to him will be raised on the last day. On All Souls' Day, we remember this promise with our own loved ones in mind, asking that God will show them mercy as we know God desires to. Prayer for the dead is a spiritual work of mercy because we offer our own love for those in need.

✦ How do you maintain hope in the Resurrection when death seems so inevitable and so final?

Brief Silence

Prayer

The psalmist writes, "You open wide your hand and satisfy the desire of every living thing" (Ps 145:16). Loving God, give us grateful hearts to receive the gifts you share, trusting you provide us with all we need. In a special way, open our hearts to the gift of yourself in this Eucharist so that we might know you more fully, love you more deeply, and serve you more faithfully in all we do. **Amen.**

THE DEDICATION OF THE LATERAN BASILICA

Today's readings assure us that we are God's temple. For those times that we have not honored the holiness that we are, we approach our God for his pardon and peace . . .

Prayer

God Most High, throughout time your people have erected buildings as a place to worship and give honor to you. Yet Paul reminds us that we, ourselves, are your temple. Recommitting ourselves to you, may we revere our own bodies—and the entirety of our being—as holy. We ask this through Christ, our Lord. **Amen**.

Gospel **John 2:13-22**

Since the Passover of the Jews was near, Jesus went up to Jerusalem. He found in the temple area those who sold oxen, sheep, and doves, as well as the money-changers seated there. He made a whip out of cords and drove them all out of the temple area, with the sheep and oxen, and spilled the coins of the money-changers and overturned their tables, and to those who sold doves he said, "Take these out of here, and stop making my Father's house a marketplace." His disciples recalled the words of Scripture, *Zeal for your house will consume me*. At this the Jews answered and said to him, "What sign can you show us for doing this?" Jesus answered and said to them, "Destroy this temple and in three days I will raise it up." The Jews said, "This temple has been under construction for forty-six years, and you will raise it up in three days?" But he was speaking about the temple of his Body. Therefore, when he was raised from the dead, his disciples remembered that he had said this, and they came to believe the Scripture and the word Jesus had spoken.

Brief Silence

For Reflection

Today's gospel reading invites us into a deeper reflection on the meaning of *church*. John's account of this episode is located at the beginning of his gospel, rather than near the end, as it is in the Synoptics. Jesus drives the money-changers and merchants out of the temple area, saying that they were making a marketplace out of the Father's house. Animal merchants and money-changers were necessary for temple function, providing the means for animal sacrifice. However, the temple ground was not to be the place for that—even in the outer Court of the Gentiles, where they had likely set up shop.

To be holy is to be *set apart*. The temple, of all places, was to be dedicated to the worship of God, a space for all people, and the noisiness of bartering crowds was an obstacle to prayer. Whether grand and ornate (like Rome's Basilica of Saint John Lateran, whose dedication we celebrate today) or intimate and humble, do our places of worship illuminate their function? Moreover, do we, by our actions in these sacred spaces, reflect the love of Christ in whose presence we stand?

✦ Which church buildings or other sacred spaces have served as a spiritual home for you? Share something about your stories there.

Brief Silence

Prayer

The psalmist writes, "You open wide your hand and satisfy the desire of every living thing" (Ps 145:16). Loving God, give us grateful hearts to receive the gifts you share, trusting you provide us with all we need. In a special way, open our hearts to the gift of yourself in this Eucharist so that we might know you more fully, love you more deeply, and serve you more faithfully in all we do. **Amen.**

THIRTY-THIRD SUNDAY IN ORDINARY TIME

Today's reading from Second Thessalonians reminds us that we must be an example of upright work for the Lord. For those times that we have fallen short of the example we are called to be, we look to God for his mercy . . .

Prayer

Lord Jesus, you have warned us about the trials that are to come in the latter days, yet sometimes it feels as if those days are already upon us. Give us the strength to trust in your word, to proclaim your name, and to persevere in spreading your love and your truth. In your name we pray. **Amen**.

Gospel **Luke 21:5-19**

While some people were speaking about how the temple was adorned with costly stones and votive offerings, Jesus said, "All that you see here—the days will come when there will not be left a stone upon another stone that will not be thrown down."

Then they asked him, "Teacher, when will this happen? And what sign will there be when all these things are about to happen?" He answered, "See that you not be deceived, for many will come in my name, saying, 'I am he,' and 'The time has come.' Do not follow them! When you hear of wars and insurrections, do not be terrified; for such things must happen first, but it will not immediately be the end." Then he said to them, "Nation will rise against nation, and kingdom against kingdom. There will be powerful earthquakes, famines, and plagues from place to place; and awesome sights and mighty signs will come from the sky.

"Before all this happens, however, they will seize and persecute you, they will hand you over to the synagogues and to prisons, and they will have you led before kings and governors because of my name. It will lead to your giving testimony. Remember, you are not to prepare your defense beforehand, for I myself shall give you a wisdom in speaking that all your adversaries will be powerless to resist or refute. You will even be handed over by parents, brothers, relatives, and friends, and they will put some of you to death. You will be hated by all because of my name, but not a hair on your head will be destroyed. By your perseverance you will secure your lives."

Brief Silence

For Reflection

In today's gospel reading, Jesus interrupts the awe-struck comments of onlookers at the monumental temple in Jerusalem to declare that not one stone of the building would be left upon another. For any Jew, the destruction of the temple, which symbolized their connection to God, by Roman imperial forces would provoke a severe crisis.

Jesus then describes cataclysmic happenings that will wreak destruction and death. He directs his listeners how to respond to these crises. If they are following him, then they too will say and do things that threaten some of the political and religious structures of their day.

First of all, he reminds his followers not to follow after anyone else; their attention must remain steadfastly on him. He speaks the same words that Gabriel spoke to Zechariah and Mary when their worlds were being turned upside down: "Do not be afraid" (Luke 1:13, 30). When disciples are seized and persecuted and handed over to the authorities because of Jesus's name, these are times to testify to the power of God. The preparation consists in persevering in a life of faithfulness and trust in the One who provoked crises by his manner of life.

✦ The devastation of the eschaton does not exist for its own sake but is to make room for God to come in and rule the earth once and for all. Where do you see God already present in the world?

Brief Silence

THIRTY-THIRD SUNDAY IN ORDINARY TIME

Prayer

The psalmist writes, "You open wide your hand and satisfy the desire of every living thing" (Ps 145:16). Loving God, give us grateful hearts to receive the gifts you share, trusting you provide us with all we need. In a special way, open our hearts to the gift of yourself in this Eucharist so that we might know you more fully, love you more deeply, and serve you more faithfully in all we do. **Amen.**

OUR LORD JESUS CHRIST, KING OF THE UNIVERSE

Today's gospel reminds us that Jesus is King precisely because he suffered for us, even though we bear the guilt. For those times that we have turned away from him, let us ask for God's pardon and peace . . .

Prayer

Lord Jesus Christ, we revere you as our King, although you did not acknowledge that title. Still we go forth rejoicing, proclaiming your name throughout the earth. In you and through you we were created, and by your love we hope to someday dwell with you in your heavenly kingdom. With trust in your promises, we pray. **Amen.**

Gospel **Luke 23:35-43**

The rulers sneered at Jesus and said, "He saved others, let him save himself if he is the chosen one, the Christ of God." Even the soldiers jeered at him. As they approached to offer him wine they called out, "If you are King of the Jews, save yourself." Above him there was an inscription that read, "This is the King of the Jews."

Now one of the criminals hanging there reviled Jesus, saying, "Are you not the Christ? Save yourself and us." The other, however, rebuking him, said in reply, "Have you no fear of God, for you are subject to the same condemnation? And indeed, we have been condemned justly, for the sentence we received corresponds to our crimes, but this man has done nothing criminal." Then he said, "Jesus, remember me when you come into your kingdom." He replied to him, "Amen, I say to you, today you will be with me in Paradise."

Brief Silence

For Reflection

Some people in Jesus's day were looking for a king like David, who would overpower imperial Roman rule and reestablish Israel's independence. And there were real advantages to monarchical rule. When Jesus appeared, proclaiming God's kingdom, he offered an antidote to imperial ways. He criticized the way the "kings of the Gentiles" lorded their power over their people and demanded recognition for their benefaction.

By contrast, he urged the leaders among his followers to be the servants of all (Luke 22:26-27), a manner of life he modeled for them as he took up his itinerant mission with people at the lowest rungs of society. Unlike a monarch who imposes harsh punishments for infractions, he instead exercised power through forgiveness and compassion when there were transgressions.

Today's gospel paints in stark contrast the power of imperial Rome, which brooks no challenges to its rule, and the "kingly" ways of Jesus that rest on forgiveness and love. Even as it appears that the former may win out, the gospel makes it utterly clear that Jesus's merciful rule cannot be extinguished by death.

✦ What does Jesus's kingship mean to you? How do you let Jesus guide and rule your life and your heart?

Brief Silence

Prayer

The psalmist writes, "You open wide your hand and satisfy the desire of every living thing" (Ps 145:16). Loving God, give us grateful hearts to receive the gifts you share, trusting you provide us with all we need. In a special way, open our hearts to the gift of yourself in this Eucharist so that we might know you more fully, love you more deeply, and serve you more faithfully in all we do. **Amen.**

CONTRIBUTORS

George J. Doyle is currently a high school campus minister at Saint Ignatius College Prep in Chicago, Illinois. Prior to this role, George served in parish ministry in Jacksonville, Florida, through the University of Notre Dame's Echo Graduate Service Program. He holds an MA in theology from Notre Dame and a BA in theology and political science from Saint John's University. An avid trumpet player and singer, George enjoys music both sacred and secular.

Katharine E. Harmon is a pastoral liturgist and American Catholic historian currently serving as associate professor of theology at Holy Cross College in Notre Dame, Indiana. A graduate of the University of Notre Dame's liturgical studies program, Harmon has contributed both scholarly and pastoral pieces on topics of liturgical renewal and American Catholic faith and practice, including *There Were Also Many Women There: Lay Women in the Liturgical Movement in the United States, 1926–59* (Liturgical Press, 2012). She resides in South Bend, Indiana, with her husband and two children.

Jessica Mannen Kimmet is a freelance writer and liturgical musician. Formerly a full-time college campus minister, she now spends her days overseeing a domestic church and the growth of her three young sons. She holds a BA in theology and music theory and a master of divinity, both from the University of Notre Dame.

Barbara E. Reid, OP, is a Dominican Sister of Grand Rapids, Michigan. She is the president of Catholic Theological Union in Chicago. She holds a PhD in biblical studies from The Catholic University of America in Washington, DC. She is the author of numerous books and is the general editor of the Wisdom Commentary series published by Liturgical Press.

Matthew Sherman serves as the director of campus ministry and associate professor of theology at Holy Cross College in Notre Dame, Indiana. His work and teaching involve the intersection of theology and ministry, the role of ethics in historical theology, and connections between sacramental and moral thought. He teaches courses in fundamental morals, bioethics, marriage and family, and Catholic social teaching.

Michele Dachtler Warner has been active in church music for most of her life, having been the first-ever cantor at her church in the early 1980s. While teaching voice lessons at Saint Mary's College (South Bend, Indiana) for many years, Michele also coached numerous leaders-of-song both with the Notre Dame Folk Choir and at workshops across the US and in Ireland. She is privileged to work and sing most often alongside her husband, Steven C. Warner.

Father Ruberval Monteiro da Silva, a Benedictine monk, was born in Rolândia in the South of Brazil. He began praying with art during his novitiate year of religious formation and later earned a doctorate in theology and Christian iconography. Fr. Monteiro da Silva has created works in churches and chapels throughout Europe and teaches liturgy and arts at the Pontifical Liturgy Institute of Rome.